STEDMAN'S POEMS.

IN UNIFORM VOLUMES.

The Blameless Prince, and other Poems. Price, $1.50.

Alice of Monmouth: An Idyl of the Great War. With other Poems. (*Third Edition.*) Price, $1.50.

Poems, Lyric and Idyllic. (*Third Edition.*) Price, $1.50.

THE BLAMELESS PRINCE,

AND OTHER POEMS.

BY

EDMUND CLARENCE STEDMAN.

BOSTON:
FIELDS, OSGOOD, & CO.,
SUCCESSORS TO TICKNOR AND FIELDS.
1869.

University Press: Welch, Bigelow, & Co.,
Cambridge.

Affectionately Inscribed

TO

RICHARD HENRY STODDARD.

Rare knowledge of our sweetest Saxon lore;
High purpose; friends, that love to seek thy door;
Strong wings of Song;—what needs a poet more?

CONTENTS.

III. SHADOW-LAND.

TRANSLATIONS FROM THEOCRITUS.

THE BLAMELESS PRINCE.

PRELUDE.

POET, wherefore hither bring
Old romance, while others sing
Sweeter idyls of to-day?
Why not picture in your lay
Western woods and waters grand,
Clouds and skies of this fair land?
Are there fairer far away?

I have many another song
Of those regions where belong,
First of all, my heart and home.
If for once my fancy roam,
Trust me, in the land I view
Falls the sunshine, falls the dew,
And the Spring and Summer come.

Why from yonder stubble glean
Ancient names of King and Queen,
  Knightly men and maidens fair?
  Are there in our time no rare
Beauteous women, heroes brave?
Is there naught this side the grave
  Worth the dust you gather there?

Nay, but these were human too,
Strong or wayward, false or true.
  Art will seek through every clime
  For her picture or her rhyme;
Yes, nor looking far around,
But to-day I sought and found
  These who lived in that old time.

Why should we again be told
Dross will mingle with all gold?
  That which time nor test can stain
  Was not smelted quite in vain.
What of Albert's blameless heart,
Arthur's old heroic part,
  Saxon Alfred's glorious reign?

Yes, my Prince was such as they,
Part of gold, and part of clay,
  Though his metal shone as bright,
  And his dross was hid from sight.
He who brightest is, and best,
Still may fear the secret test
  That shall try his heart aright.

Let me, then, begin my lay
In such English as I may.
  Turn the leaf that lies between
  You who listen and the scene!
Your pity for the Lady, since
She died of sorrow; spare my Prince;
  Love to the last my gentle Queen!

THE BLAMELESS PRINCE.

LONG since, there was a Princess of the blood,
  Sole heiress to the crown her father wore, —
Plucked from a dying stem, that one fair bud
  Put forth, and withered ere it others bore ;
And scarce the King her blossomed youth had seen,
When he, too, slept the sleep, and she was Queen.

Hers was a goodly realm, not stretched afar
  In desert wilds by wolf and savage scoured,
But locked in generous limits, strong in war,
  Serene in peace, with mountains walled and towered,
Fed by the tilth of many a fertile plain,
And veined with streams that proudly sought the main.

The open sea bore commerce to her marts,
  Tumbling half round her borders with its tide;
Her vessels shot the surge ; all noble arts
  Of use and beauty in her towns were plied;
Her court was regal ; lords and ladies lit
The palace with their graces and their wit.

Wise councillors devised each apt decree
  That gained the potent sanction of her hand;
Great captains led her arms on shore and sea;
  She was the darling of a loyal land;
Poets sang her praises, and in hut and hall
Her excellence was the discourse of all.

Her pride was suited to her high estate,
  Her gentleness was equal with her youth,
Her wisdom in her goodness found its mate;
  Her beauty was not that which brings to ruth
Men's lives, but clear and luminous; — and fair
Her locks, and over all a sovereign air.

Without, she bore herself as rulers should,
  Queenly in walk and gesture and attire;
Within, she nursed her flower of maidenhood,
  Sweet girlish thoughts and virginal desire;
No woman's head so keen to work its will
But that the woman's heart is mistress still.

Three years she ruled a nation well content
  To have a maiden queen; then came a day
When those on whom her councils chiefly leant
  Began to speak of marriage, and to pray
Their sovereign not to hold herself alone,
Nor trust the tenure of an heirless throne;

And then the people took the cry, nor lack
  Was there of courtly suitors far or near, —
Kings, dukes, crown-princes, — swift upon the track
  Like huntsmen closing round a royal deer.
These she regarded not, but still, among
Her maids and missals to her freedom clung.

And with the rest there came a puissant king,
Whose country pressed against her own domain, —
In strength its equal, but continuing
Its dearest foe through many a martial reign.
He sued to join his hand and realm with hers,
And end these wars ; then all her ministers

Pleaded his suit ; but, asking yet for grace,
And that her hand might wait upon her heart,
She halted, till the proud king turned his face
Homeward ; and still the people, for their part,
Waited her choice, nor grudged her sex's share
Of coyness to a queen so young and fair.

There was a little State that nestled close
Beside her boundaries, as wont to claim,
Though free, protection there from outer foes,
A Principality — at least in name —
Whose ruler was her father's life-long friend
And ally, skilled in statesmancraft to lend

Shrewd counsel, and who made, in days gone by,
  A visit to this court, and with him led
His son, a gentle Prince, of years anigh
  Her own, — twelve summers shone from either head;
And while their elders moved from place to place, —
The field-review, the audience, the chase, —

The Princess and the Prince, together thrown,
  With their companions held a mimic court,
And with that sweet equality, the crown
  Of Childhood, — which discovers in its sport
No barriers of rank or wealth or power, —
He named himself her consort. From that hour

The mindful Princess never quite forgot
  Those joyous days, nor him, the fair-haired Prince;
And though she well had learned her greater lot,
  And haply from his thought had passed long since
Her girlish image, chance, that moves between
Two courts, had brought his portrait to the Queen.

This from her cabinet she took one morn,
  When they still urged the suit of that old king,
And said, half-jesting, with a pretty scorn,
  "Why mate your wilful Queen with mouldering
And crabbed Age? Now were he shaped like this,
With such a face, he were not so amiss.

"Queens are but women; 't is a sickly year
  That couples frost and thaw, our minstrels sing."—
"Ho!" thought the graybeards, "sets the wind so near?"
  And thought again: "Why not?" the schemeful king
Perchance would rule us where he should be ruled;
A humbler consort will be sooner schooled."

Forewarned are those whom Fortune's gifts await.
  Ere waned a moon the elder prince had learned—
From half the weathercocks which gilt the state,
  Spying the wind and shifting where it turned—
That for love's simple sake his son could gain
The world's chief prize, which kings had sought in vain.

How could he choose but clutch it? Yet the son
  Seemed worthy, for his parts were of that mould
Oft-failing Nature strives to join in one,
  And shape a hero — pure and wise and bold:
In arts and arms the wonder of his peers,
The flower of princes, prince of cavaliers;

Tall, lithe of form, and of a northern mien,
  Gentle in speech and thought, — while thus he shone,
A rising star, though chosen of a queen,
  Why seek the skies less tranquil than his own?
Why should he climb beside her perilous height,
And in that noonday blaze eclipse his light?

Ah, why? — one's own life may be bravely led,
  But not another's. Yet, as to and fro
The buzzing private embassies were sped,
  And when the Queen's own pages, bowing low,
Told in his ear a sweet and secret story,
The Prince, long trained to seek his house's glory,

Let every gracious sentence seem a plume
  Of love and beckoning beauty for his helm.
So passed a season ; then the cannon's boom
  And belfry's peal delivered to the realm
The Queen's betrothal, and the councils met,
And for the nuptial rites a day was set.

NOW when the time grew ripe, the favored Prince
  Rides forth, and through the little towns that mourn
His loss, and past the boundaries ; and, since
  To ape the pomp to which he was not born
Seemed in his soul a foolish thing and vain,
A few near comrades, only, made his train.

Nor pressed the populace along the ways;
  But — for he wished it so — unheralded
He rode from post to post through many days,
  Yet gained a greatness as the distance fled,
As some dim comet, drawing near its bound,
Takes lustre from the orb it courses round.

And league by league his fantasies outran
  His progress, brooding on his mistress' power,
Until his own estate the while began
  To seem of lesser worth each passing hour;
And with misdoubt this fortune weighed him down,
As though a splendid mantle had been thrown

About him, which he knew not well to wear,
  And might not forfeit. Yet he spurred apace,
And reached a country-seat that bordered near
  The Capital. Here, for a little space,
He was to rest from travel, and await
His day of entrance at the city's gate.

Upon these grounds a gray-haired noble dwelt,
  A ribboned courtier of the former reign;
A tedious proper man, who glibly knelt
  To royalty, — this ancient chamberlain, —
Yoked with a girlish wife, and, for the rest,
Proud of the charge that made a prince his guest.

The highway ran beside a greenwood keep
  That reached, herefrom, quite to the city's edge;
Across, the fields with golden corn were deep;
  The level sunset pierced the wayside hedge;
The banks were all abloom; — a pheasant whirred
Far in the bush; anon, some tuneful bird

Broke into song, or, from a covert dark,
  A bounding deer its dappled haunches showed
As though it heard the staghound's distant bark.
  The wistful Prince with loitering purpose bode,
And thought how good it were to spend one's life
Far off from men, nor jostled with their strife.

Even as he mused he saw his host ahead,
  Speeding to welcome him, in lordly wont,
And all the household in a line bestead ;
  And lightly with that escort, at the front,
A peerless woman rode across the green ;
Then the Prince thought, "It surely is the Queen,

Who comes to meet me of her loving grace!"
  And his blood mounted; but he knew how fair
The royal locks, and, when she neared his place,
  He saw the lady's prodigal dark hair
And wondrous loveliness were wide apart
From the sweet, tranquil picture next his heart.

And when the chamberlain, with halted suit,
  Made reverence, and was answered courteous-wise,
The lady to her knightly guest's salute
  Turned her face full, so that he marked her eyes, —
How dewy gray beneath each long, black lid,
And danger somewhere in their light lay hid.

There are some natures housed so chaste within
  Their placid dwellings that their heads control
The tumult of their hearts; and thus they win
  A quittance from this pleading of the soul
For Love, whose service does so wound and heal;
How should they crave for what they cannot feel?

From passion and from pain enfranchised quite,
  Alike from gain and never-stanched Regret,
Calm as the blind who have not seen the light,
  The dumb who hear no precious voice, and yet
The sun forever pours his lambent fire
And the high winds are vocal with desire.

And there are those whose fervent souls are wed
  To glorious bodies, panoplied for love,
Born to hear sweetest words that can be said,
  To give and gather kisses, and to move
All men with longing after them, — to know
What flowers of paradise for lovers grow.

The Vestal, with her silvery content,
  The Lesbian, with the passion and the pain,—
Which creature hath their one Creator lent
  More light of heaven? Who would dare restrain
The beams of either? who the radiance mar
Of the white planet or the burning star?

If in its innocence a life is bound
  With cords that thrall its birthright and design,
Let those whose hands the evil meshes wound
  Pray that it cast no look beyond their line;
That no strong voice too late may enter in
Its prison-range, to teach what might have been.

Was there no conscious spirit thus to plead
  For this bright lady, as the wondering guest
Closed with his welcomers, and each took heed
  Of each, and horse to horse they rode abreast,
Nearing a fair and spacious house that stood,
Half hidden, in the edges of the wood?

And while, the last court-tidings running o'er,
Their talk on this and that at random fell,
And the trains joined behind, the lady bore
Her beauteous head askance, yet wist full well
How the Prince looked and spoke ; unwittingly,
With the strange female sense and secret eye,

Made of him there her subtle estimate,
Forecast his lot, and thought how all things flow
To those who have a surfeit. Could the great,
The perfect Queen, she marvelled, truly know
And love him at his value ? In his turn,
He read her face as 't were a marble urn

Embossed with Truth and blushful Innocence,
Yet with the wild Loves carven in repose ;
And as he looked he felt, and knew not whence,
A thought like this come as the wind that blows,
" A face to lose one's life for ; ay, and more,
To live for ! " — So they reached the sculptured door

And casements gilded with the dying light.
  That eve the host spread out a stately board,
And with his household far into the night
  Feasted the Prince. The lady, next her lord,
Drooped like a musk-rose trained beside a tomb.
Loath was the guest that night to seek his room.

AH! wherefore tell again an oft-told tale, —
  That of the sleeping knight who lost his wage
In the enchanted land, though cased with mail,
  And bore the sacred shrine an empty gage?
How this thing went it were not worth to view
But for the triple coil which thence outgrew;

How, with the morn, the ancient chamberlain
  Made off, and on the marriage business moved;
How day by day those young hearts fed amain
  Upon the food of lovers, till — they loved.
Beneath the mists of duty and degree
A warmth of passion crept deliciously

About the twain; and there, within the gleam
  Of those gray languid eyes, his nearing fate
Seemed to the one a far, unquiet dream.
  So when the heralds said, "All things await
Your princely coming," the glad summons broke
Upon him like a harsh bell's jangling stroke,

And waked him, and he knew he must be gone
  And put that honeyed chalice quite away;
Yet once more met the lady, and alone,
  It chanced, within the grounds. The two, that day,
Lured by a falling water's sound, went deep
Beyond the sunlight, in the forest-keep.

Here from a range of wooded uplands leapt
  A mountain brook and far-off meadows sought;
Now under firs and tasselled chestnuts crept,
  Then on through jagged rocks a passage fought,
Until it clove this shadowy gorge and cool
In one white cataract, — with a dark, broad pool

Beneath, the home of mottled trout. One side
  Rose the cliff's hollowed height, and overhung
An open sward across that basin wide.
  The liberal sun through slanting larches flung
Rich spots of gold upon the tufted ground,
And the great royal forest gloomed around.

The Prince, divided from the world so far,
  Sat with the lady on a fallen tree;
They looked like lovers, yet a prison-bar
  Between them had not made the two less free.
Only their eyes told what they could not say,
For still their lips spoke alien words that day.

She told a legend of an early king
  Who knew the fairy of this wildwood glen,
And often sought her haunt, far off to fling
  His grandeur, and be loved like common men.
He died long since, the lady said; but she,
Who could not die, how weary she must be!

They talked of the strange beauty of the spot,
  The light that glinted through the ancient trees,
Their own young lives, the Prince's future lot;
  Then jested with false laughs. Like tangled bees,
Each other and themselves they sweetly stung;
They sung fond songs, and mocked the words they sung.

At last he hung his picture by a chain
  About her neck, and on it graved the date.
Her merry eyes grew soft with tender pain;
  She heard him sigh, "Alas, by what rude fate
Our lives, like ships at sea, an instant meet,
Then part forever on their courses fleet!"

And in sheer pity of herself she dropped
  Her lovely head; and, though with self she strove,
One hot tear fell. The shadow, which had stopped
  On her life's dial, moved again, and Love
Went sobbing by, and only left his wraith;
For both were loyal to their given faith.

Farewells they breathed and self-reproaches found,
  Half gliding with the current to the fall,
Yet struggling for the shore. Was she not bound?
  Did not his plighted future, like a wall,
Jut 'cross the stream? They feared themselves, and rose,
And through the forest gained the mansion-close

Unmissed, and parted thus, nor met anew;
  For on the morrow, when the Prince took horse,
The lady feigned an illness, or 't was true, —
  Yet maybe from her oriel marked his course,
Watching his plume, that into distance past,
Like some dear sail which sinks from sight at last.

He rode beneath their arch, where pennons flared
And standards with his colors blazoned in.
Then thousands shouted welcome; trumpets blared;
He felt the glories of his life begin!
Far, far behind, that eddy in its stream
Now seemed; its vanished shores, in turn, a dream.

Enough; he passed the ways and reached the Queen.
With pomp and pageantry the vows were said.
Leave to the chroniclers the storied scene,
The church, the court, the masks and jousts that sped;
Not theirs, but ours, to follow Love apart,
Where first the bridegroom held his bride to heart,

And saw her purity and regnant worth
Thus kept for him and yielded to his care.
What marvel that of all who dwelt on earth
He seemed most fortunate and she most fair
That self-same hour? And "By God's grace," he thought,
"May I to some ignoble end be brought,

"Unless I so reward her for her choice,
  And shape my future conduct in this land
By her deserving, that the world's great voice
  Proclaim me not unworthy! Let my hand
Henceforward make her tasks its own, — my life
Be merged in this fair ruler, precious wife,

"The paragon and glory of her kind!"
  Who reads his own heart will not think it strange
He put that yester romance from his mind
  So readily. Men's lives, like oceans, change
In shifting tides, and ebb from either shore
Till the strong planet draws them on once more.

AND as a pilgrim, shielded by the wings
Of some bright angel, crosses perilous ground,
Through unknown ways, and, while she leads and sings,
Forgets the past, nor sees what pits surround
His footsteps, so the young Prince cast away
That self-distrust, and with his sovereign May

The gladness joined, and with her sat in state,
Beneath the ancient scutcheons of her throne,
And welcome gave, and led the revels late;
But when the still and midnight heavens shone
They fled the masquers, and the city's hum
Was silent, and the palace halls grew dumb,

And Love and Sleep in that serene eclipse
Moved, making prince and clown of one degree.
Then was she all his own; then from her lips
He learned with what a sweet humility
She, whose least word a spacious kingdom ruled,
In Love's free vassalage would fain be schooled.

How poor, she said, her sovereignty seemed,
  Unless it made her richer in his eye!
And poor his life, until her sunlight beamed
  Upon it, said the Prince. So months went by;
They were a gracious pair; the Queen was glad;
Peace smiled, and the wide land contentment had.

And for a time the courteous welcome paid
  The chosen consort, and the people's joy
In the Queen's joy, kept silent those who weighed
  The Prince's make, and sought to find alloy
In his fine gold; but, when the freshness fled
From these things told, some took new thought and said:

"Look at the Queen: her heart is wholly set
  Upon the Prince! what if he warp her mind
To errant policies, and rule us yet
  By proxy?" "What and if he prove the kind
Of trifling gallant," others said, "to slight
Our mistress, for each new and base delight?

"Ay, we will watch him, lest he do her wrong!"
  And his due station, even from the first,
The peers of haughty rank and lineage long,
  Jealous of one whose blossom at a burst
Outflamed their own, begrudged him; till their pique
Grew plain, and sent proud color to his cheek.

So now he fared as some new actor fares,
  Who through dark arras gains the open boards,
Facing the lights, and feels a thousand stares
  Come full upon him; and the great throng hoards
Its plaudits; and, as he begins his tale,
His rivals wait to mock him if he fail.

But here a brave simplicity of soul
  And careless vigilance, by honor bred,
Stayed him, and o'er his actions held control.
  A host of generous virtues stood in stead
To help him on; with patient manliness
He kept his rank, no greater and no less;

His life was as a limpid rivulet;
  His thoughts, like golden sands, were through it seen,
Not on himself in poor ambition set,
  But on his chosen country and the Queen;
And with such gentle tact he bore a sense
Of conduct due, nor took nor gave offence,

That, as time went, he earned their trust, who first
  Withheld it him, and brought them, one by one,
To seek him for a comrade; but he nursed
  His friendships with such equal care that none
Could claim him as their own; nor was his word
Of counsel dulled by being often heard;

Nor would he sully his fresh youth among
  The roisterers and pretty wanton dames
Who strove to win him; nor with ribald tongue
  Joined in the talk that round a palace flames;
Nor came and went alone, save — 't was his wont
In his own land, — he haply left the hunt

On forest days, and, plunging down the wood,
  There in the brakes and copses half forgot
The part he bore, and caught anew the mood
  Of youth, and felt a heart for any lot;
Then, loitering cityward behind the train,
With fresher courage took his place again

His pure life made the wits about the court
  Find in its very blamelessness a fault
That lacked the generous failings of their sort.
  "With so much sweet," they swore, "a grain of salt
Were welcome! lighter tongue and freer mood
Were something more of man, if less of prude!"

And others to his praises would oppose
  Suspicion of his prowess, and they said,
"Our rose of princes is a thornless rose,
  A woman's toy!" and, when the months were sped,
And the glad Queen was childed with a son,
Light jests upon his mission well begun

They bandied; yet the Prince, who felt the sting,
  Bided his time. Till on the land there brake
A sudden warfare; for that haughty king,
  Gathering a mighty armament to take
Revenge for his lost suit, with sword and flame
Against the borders on short pretext came.

Then with hot haste the Queen's whole forces poured
  To meet him. With the call to horse and blade
The Prince, deep-chafed in spirit, placed his sword
  At orders of the General, and prayed
A humble station, but, as due his rank,
Next in command was made, and led the flank.

And so with doubtful poise a fierce war raged,
  Till on a day encountered face to face
The two chief hosts, and dreadful battle waged
  To close the issue. In its opening space
Death smote the General, and in tumult sore
The line sank back; but swiftly, at the fore

Placing himself, the Prince right onward hurled
  The strife once more, and with his battle-shout
Woke victory; again his forces whirled
  The hostile troops, and drove them on in rout.
The strength of ten battalions seemed to yield
Before his arm; and so he won that field,

And slew with his own hand the vengeful king,
  And with that death-stroke brought the war to end,
Conquering the common foe, and conquering
  The hate, from which he would not else defend
His clear renown than with such manful deeds
As fall to faith and valor at their needs.

Again — this time the chaplet was his own —
  The people wreathed their laurels for his brow;
His horses trod on flowers; the city shone
  With flags of victory, and none but now —
As with no vaunting mien he wore his bays —
Confessed him brave as good, and gave their praise.

PEACE smiled anew ; the kingdom was at rest.
Ah, happy Queen ! whom every matron's tongue
Ran envious of, with such a consort blest
As wins the heart of women, old and young ;
So gallant, yet so good, the gentlest maid
By this fair standard her own suitor weighed.

I hold the perfect mating of two souls,
Through wedded love, to be the sum of bliss.
When Earth, this fruit that ripens as it rolls
In sunlight, grows more prime, lives will not miss
Their counterparts, and each shall find its own ;
But now with what blind chance the lots are thrown !

And because Love sets with a rising tide
  Along the drift where much has gone before
One holds of worth, — we lavish first, beside,
  Heart, honors, regal gifts, and love the more
When yielding most, — for this the Queen's love knew
No slack, but still its current deeper grew.

And because Love is free, and follows not
  On gratitude, nor comes from what is given
So much as on the giving; and, I wot,
  Partly because it irks one to have thriven
At hands which seem the weaker, and should thrive
While those of him they cling to lift and strive;

And partly that his marriage seemed a height
  Which raised him from the passions of our kind,
Nor with his own intent; and that, despite
  Its clear repose, he somehow longed to find
The lower world, starve, hunger, and be fed
With joy and sorrow, sweet and bitter bread, —

For all these things the Prince loved not the Queen
  With that sufficience which alone can take
A rapture in itself and rest serene;
  Yet knew not what his life lacked that should make
It worth to live, — our custom has such art
To dull the craving of the famished heart, —

Perchance had never known it, but a light
  Flashed in his path and lit a fiery train
About him; else, day following day, and night
  By night, through years his soul had felt no pain,
No triumph, but had shared the common lull,
Been all it seemed, as blameless, true, and dull.

And yet in one fair woman beauty, youth,
  And passion were united, and her love
Was framed about his likeness. Some, forsooth,
  May shift their changeful worship as they rove,
Or clowns or princes; but her fancy slept,
Dreaming upon that picture which she kept,

A secret pain and pleasance. With what strife
  Men sought her love she wist not, for the prize
Was not for them. She lived a duteous life.
  'T was something thus to let her constant eyes
Feed on his face, to hear his name, — to know
He lived, had walked those paths, had loved her so.

There is a painting of a youthful monk
  Who sits within a walled and cloistered nook,
His breviary closed, and listens, sunk
  In day-dreams, to a viol, — with a look
Of strange regret fixed on two pairing doves,
Who find their fate and simple natural loves.

Yet bonds of gold, linked hands, and chancel vows,
  Even spousal beds, do not a marriage make.
When such things chain the soul that never knows
  Love's mating, little vantage shall it take,
Wandering with alien feet throughout the wide,
Hushed temple, over those who pine outside!

So this young wife forecast her horoscope
  And found its wedded lines of little worth,
Yet owned not to herself what hopeless hope
  Or dumb intent made green her spot of earth.
So passed three changeless years, as such years be;
At last the old lord died, and left her free,

The mistress of his rank and broad estate,
  In honor of her constancy. Then life
Rushed back; she saw her beauty grown more great,
  Ripened as if a summer field were rife
With grain, the harvester neglectful, since
Hers was no mean desire that sought a prince,

Eager to make his birth and bloom her own,
  Or reign a wanton favorite. But she thought,
"I might have loved and clung to him alone,
  Am fairer than he knew me; yet, if aught
Of rarity make sweet my hair and lips,
What sweetness hath the honey that none sips?"

After her time of mourning she grew bold
  And said, "Once let me look upon his face!
The Queen will take no harm if I behold
  What all the world can see." She left her place,
And with a kinsman, at a palace rout,
Followed the long line passing in and out

Before the dais. The Prince's eyes and hers
  Met like the clouds that lighten. In a breath
Swift memory flamed between them, as, when stirs
  No wind, and the dark sky is still as death,
One lance of living fire is hurled across;
Then comes the whirlwind, and the forests toss!

Yet as she bent her beauteous shoulders down,
  And heard the kindly greeting of the Queen,
He spoke such words as one who wears a crown
  Speaks, and no more; and with a low, proud mien
She murmured answer, from the presence past
Lightly, nor any look behind her cast.

In that first glimpse each read the other's heart;
  But not without a summoning of himself
To judgment did the Prince forever part
  From truth and fealty. As he pondered, still
With stronger voice Love claimed a debt unpaid,
And youth's hot pulses would not be gainsaid.

She with a fierce, full gladness saw again
  Their broken threads of love begin to spin
In one red strand, and let it guide her then,
  Whether it led to danger or to sin;
And shortly, on the morrow, took the road,
And gained her country-seat, and there abode.

The Prince, a bright near morning, mounted horse,
  Garbed for the hunt, and left the town, and through
The deep-pathed wood rode on a wayward course,
  With a set purpose in him, — though he knew
It not, and let his steed go where it might;
For this sole thought pursued him since that night: —

"What recompense for me who have not sown
The seed and reaped the harvest of my days?
Youth passes like a bird; but love alone
Makes wealth of riches, power of rank, men's praise
A goodly sound. Of such things have I aught?
There is a foil to make their substance naught.

"What were his gifts who made each lovely thing,
Yet lacked the gift of love? or what the fame
Of some dwarfed poet, whose numbers still we sing,
If no fair woman trembled where he came?
The beggar dying in ditch is not accurst
If love once crowned him! Fate may do her worst.

"For Age that erst has drawn the wine of love
And filled its birth-cup to the jewelled brim,
And, while it sparkled, held it high above,
And drained it slowly, swiftly,—then, though dim
Grow the blurred eyes, and comfort and desire
Are but the ashes of their ancient fire,

"Yet will it bide its exit in content,
Remembering the past, nor grudge, with hoar
And ravenous look, the youth we have not spent.
No earthly sting has power to harm it more;
It lived and loved, was young, and now is old,
And life is rounded like a ring of gold."

Thereat with sudden rein the Prince wheeled horse,
And sought a pathway that he long had known
Yet shunned till now. Beside a water-course
It led him for a winding league and lone;
Then made a rugged circuit, — where the brook
Down a steep ledge of rock its plunges took, —

And ended at an open sward, the same
Against whose edge the leaping cataract fell
From those high cliffs. Five years ago he came
To bury youth and love within that dell,
And, as again he reached the spot he sought,
Truth, fame, his child, the Queen, were all as naught.

Dismounting then, he pushed afoot, between
The alder saplings, to the outer wood,
The grounds, the garden-walks, and found, unseen,
A private door, nor tarried till he stood
Within the threshold of my Lady's room, —
A shadowed nook, all stillness and perfume.

Jasmine and briony the lattice climbed,
The rose and honeysuckle trailed above;
'T was such an hour as poets oft have rhymed,
And such a chamber as all lovers love.
He found her there, and at her footstool knelt.
Each in the other's fancies had so dwelt,

That, as one sees for days a sweet strange face,
Until at night in dreams he does caress
Its owner, and next morning in some place
Meets her, and wonders if she too can guess
How near and known he thinks her, — in this wise
They read one story in each other's eyes.

Her thick hair falling from its lilies hid
Their first long kiss of passion and content.
He heard her soft, glad murmur, as she slid
Within his hold, and 'gainst his bosom leant,
Whispering: "At last! at last! the years were sore."
"Their spite," he said, "shall do us wrong no more!"

What else, when mingled longings swell full-tide,
And the heart's surges leap their bounds for aye,
And fell the landmarks? What but fate defied,
Time clutched, and any future held at bay?
They recked not of the thorn, but seized the flower;
For all the sin, their joy was great that hour.

And since, for all the joy, theirs was a sin
That baned them with one bane; since many men
Had sought her love, but one alone could win
That largess, with his blameless life till then
Inviolate; — they bargained for love's sake
No severance of their covert league to make.

Yet, since nobility compelled them still,
  They pledged themselves for honor's sake to hold
This hidden unto death; at either's will
  To meet and part in secret; to infold
In their own hearts their trespass and delight,
Nor look their love, but guard it day or night.

SO fell the blameless Prince. That day more late
  Than wont he reached the presence of the Queen,
Deep in a palace chamber, where she sate
  Fondling his child. The sunset lit her mien,
And made a saintly glory in her hair;
An awe came on him as he saw her there.

And, because perfect love suspecteth not,
  She found no blot upon his brow. 'T was good
To take a pleasure in her wedded lot,
  And watch the infant creeping where he stood;
And, as he bent his head, she little wist
What kisses burned upon the lips she kissed.

And he, still kind and wise in his decline,
  Seeing her trustful calm, had little heart
To shake it. So his conduct gave no sign
  Of broken faith; no slurring of his part
Betrayed him to the courtiers or the wife.
Perhaps a second spring-time in his life

Waxed green, and fresh-bloomed love renewed again
  The joys that light our youth and leave our prime,
And women found him tenderer, and men
  A blither, heartier comrade; but, meantime,
What hidden gladness made his visage bright
They could not guess; nor with what craft and sleight

The paramours, in fealty to that Love
  Who laughs at locks and walks in hooded guise,
Met here and there, yet made no careless move,
  Nor bared their strategy to cunning eyes.
And though, a portion of the winter year,
The Queen's own summons brought her rival near

The Prince, among the ladies of her train,
  Then, meeting face to face at morn and night,
They were as strangers. If it was a pain
  To pass so coldly on, in love's despite,
It was a joy to hear each other's tone,
And keep the life-long secret still their own.

Once having dipped their palms they drank full draught,
  And, like the desert-parched, alone at first
Felt the delight of drinking, while they quaffed
  As if the waters could not slake their thirst;
That nicer sense unreached, when down we fling,
And view the green oasis round the spring.

And, in that first bewilderment, perchance
  The Prince's lapse had caught some peering eye,
But that his long repute, and maintenance
  Against each test, had put suspicion by.
Now no one watched or doubted him. So long
His inner strength had made his outwork strong,

So long had smoothed his face, 't was light to take,
  From what had been his blamelessness, a mask.
And still, for honor's and the country's sake,
  He set his hands to every noble task;
Held firmly yet his place among the great,
Won by the sword and saviour of the state;

And as in war, so now in civic peace,
  He led the people on to higher things,
And fostered Art and Song, and brought increase
  Of Knowledge, gave to Commerce broader wings,
And with his action strengthened fourfold more
The weight his precept in their councils bore.

Then as the mellow years their fruitage brought,
  And fair strong children made secure the throne,
He reared them wisely, heedfully; and sought
  Their good, the Queen's desire, and these alone.
Himself so pure, that fathers bade their sons,
"Observe the Prince, who every license shuns;

"Who, being most brave, is purest!" Wedded wives,
  Happy themselves, the Queen still happiest found,
And plighted maids still wished their lovers' lives
  Conformed to his. Such manhood wrapt him round,
So winsome were his grace and knightly look,
The dames at court their lesser spoil forsook,

And wove a net to snare him, and their mood
  Grew warmer for his coldness; and the hearts
Of those most heartless beat with quicker blood,
  Foiled of his love; yet, heedless of their arts,
Courteous to all, he went his way content,
Nor ever from his princely station bent.

"What is this charm," they asked, "that makes him
chaste
Beyond all men?" and wist not what they said.
The common folk, — because the Prince had cased
His limbs in silver mail, and on his head
Worn snowy plumes, and, covered thus in white,
Shone in the fiercest turmoil of the fight;

And mostly for the whiteness of his soul,
Which seemed so virginal and all unblurred, —
They called him the White Prince, and through the whole
True land the name became a household word.
"God save the Queen!" the loyal people sung,
"And the White Prince!" came back from every tongue.

So passed the stages of a glorious reign.
The Queen in tranquil goodness reached her noon;
The Prince wore year by year his double chain;
His mistress kept her secret like the moon,
That hides one half its splendor and its shade;
And newer times and men their entrance made.

But did these two, who took their secret fill
  Of stolen waters, find the greater bliss
They sought? At first, to meet and part at will
  Was, for the peril's sake, a happiness;
Ay, even the sense of guilt made such delights
More worth, as one we call the wisest writes.

But with the later years Time brought about
  His famed revenges. Not that love grew cold,
The lady never found a cause to doubt
  That with the Prince his passion kept its hold;
And while their loved are loyal to them yet,
'T is not the wont of women to regret.

Yet 't was her lot to live as one whose wealth
  Is in another's name; to sigh at fate
That hedged her from possession, save by stealth
  And trespass on the guileless Queen's estate;
To see her lover farthest when most near,
Nor dare before the world to make him dear.

To see her perfect beauty but a lure,
  That made men list to follow where she went,
And kneel to woo the hand they deemed so pure,
  And hunger for her pitying mouth's consent;
Calling her hard, who was so gently made,
Nor found delight in all their homage paid.

Nor ever yet was woman's life complete
  Till at her breast the child of him she loved
Made life and love one name. Though love be sweet,
  And passing sweet, till then its growth has proved
In woman's paradise a sterile tree,
Fruitless, though fair its leaves and blossoms be.

Meanwhile the Prince put on his own disguise
  Holding it naught for what it kept secure,
Nor wore it only in his comrades' eyes;
  Beneath this cloak and seeming to be pure
He felt the thing he seemed. For some brief space
His conscience took the reflex of his face.

But lastly through his heart there crept a sense
  Of falseness, like a worm about the core,
Until he grew to loathe the long pretence
  Of blamelessness, and would the mask he wore
By some swift judgment from his face were torn,
So might the outer quell the inner scorn.

Such self-contempt befell him, when the feast
  Rang with his praise, he blushed from nape to crown,
And ground his teeth in silence, yet had ceased
  To bear it, crying, "Crush me not quite down,
Who ask your scorn, as viler than you deem
Your vilest, and am nothing that I seem!"

With such a cry his conscience riotous
  Had thrown, perchance, the burden on it laid,
But love and pity held his voice; and thus
  The paramours their constant penance made·
False to themselves, before the world a lie,
Yet each for each had cast the whole world by.

In those transcendent moments, when the fire
  Leapt up between them rapturous and bright
One incompleteness bred a wild desire
  To let the rest have token of its light;
So natural seemed their love, — so hapless, too,
They might not make it glorious to view,

And speak their joy. 'T was all as they had come,
  They two, in some far wildwood wandering mazed,
Upon a mighty cataract, whose foam
  And splendor ere that time had never dazed
Men's eyes, nor any hearing save their own
Could listen to its immemorial moan,

And felt amid their triumph bitter pain
  That only for themselves was spread that sight.
Oft, when his comrades sang a tender strain,
  And music, talk, and wine, outlasted night,
Rose in the Prince's throat this sudden tide,
"And I, — I also know where Love doth hide!"

Yet still the seals were ever on his mouth ;
  No heart, save one, his joy and dole might share.
Passed on the winter's rain and summer's drouth ;
  Friends more and more, and lovers true, the pair,
Though life its passion and its youth had spent,
Still kept their faith as seasons came and went.

ONE final hour, with stammering voice and halt,
  The Prince said: "Dear, for you,—whose only gain
Was in your love that made such long default
  To self,—Heaven deems you sinless! but a pain
Is on my soul, and shadow of guilt threefold:
First, in your fair life, fettered by my hold;

"Then in the ceaseless wrong I do the Queen,
Who worships me, unknowing; worse than all,
To wear before the world this painted mien!
See to it: on my head some bolt will fall!
We have sweet memories of the good years past,
Now let this secret league no longer last."

So of her love and pure unselfishness
She yielded at his word, yet fain would pray
For one more tryst, one day of tenderness,
Where first their lives were mated. Such a day
Found them intwined together, met to part,
Lips pressed to lips, and voiceless grief at heart.

And last the Prince drew off his signet-stone,
And gave it to his mistress, — as he rose
To shut the book of happy moments gone,
For so all earthly pleasures find a close, —
Yet promised, at her time of utmost need
And summons by that token, to take heed

And do her will. "And from this hour," he said,
  "No woman's kiss save one my lips shall know."
So left her pale and trembling there, and fled,
  Nor looked again, resolved it must be so;
But somewhere gained his horse, and through the wood
Moved homeward with his thoughts, a phantom brood

That turned the long past over in his mind,
  Poising its good and evil, while a haze
Gathered around him, of that sombre kind
  Which follows from a place where many days
Have seen us go and come; and even if sore
Has been our sojourn there, we feel the more

That parting is a sorrow, — though we part
  With those who loved us not, or go forlorn
From pain that ate its canker in the heart;
  But when we leave the paths where Love has borne
His garlands to us, Pleasure poured her wine,
Where life was wholly precious and divine,

Then go we forth as exiles. In such wise
  The loathful Prince his homeward journey made,
Brooding, and marked not with his downcast eyes
  The shadow that within the coppice shade
Sank darker still ; but at the horse's gait
Kept slowly on, and rode to meet his fate

For from the west a silent gathering drew,
  And hid the summer sky, and brought swift night
Across that shire, and went devouring through
  The strong old forest, stronger in its might.
With the first sudden crash the Prince's steed
Took the long stride, and galloped at good need.

The wild pace tallied with the rider's mood,
  And on he spurred, and even now had reached
The storm that charged the borders of the wood,
  When one great whirlwind seized an oak which bleached
Across his path, and felled it ; and its fall
Bore down the Prince beneath it, horse and all.

There lay he as he fell; but the mad horse
  Plunged out in fright, and reared upon his feet,
And for the city struck a headlong course,
  With clatter of hoof along the central street,
Nor halted till, thus masterless and late,
Bleeding and torn, he reached the palace-gate.

Then rose a clamor and the tidings spread,
  And servitors and burghers thronged about,
Crying, "The Prince's horse! the Prince is dead!"
  Till on the courser's track they sallied out,
And came upon the fallen oak, and found
The Prince sore maimed and senseless on the ground.

Then wattling boughs, they raised him in their hold,
  And after that rough litter, and before,
The people went in silence; but there rolled
  A fiery vapor from the lights they bore,
Like some red serpent huge along the road.
Even thus they brought him back to his abode.

There the pale Queen fell on him at the porch,
  Dabbling her robes in blood, and made ado,
And over all his henchman held a torch,
  Until with reverent steps they took him through;
And the doors closed, and midnight from the domes
Was sounded, and the people sought their homes.

But on the morrow, like a dreadful bird,
  Flew swift the tidings of this sudden woe,
And reached the Prince's paramour, who heard
  Aghast, as one who crieth loud, "The blow
Is fallen! I am the cause!" — as one who saith,
"Now let me die, whose hands have given death!"

So gat her to the town remorsefully,
  White with a mortal tremor and the sin
Which sealed her mouth, and waited what might be,
  And watched the doors she dared not pass within.
Alas, poor lady! that lone week of fears
Outlived the length of all her former years.

Some days the Prince, upon the skirts of death,
  Spake not a word nor heard the Queen's one prayer,
Nor turned his face, nor felt her loving breath,
  Nor saw his children when they gathered there,
But rested dumb and motionless; and so
The Queen grew weak with watching and her woe,

Till from his bed they bore her to her own
  A little. In the middle-tide of night,
Thereafter, he awoke with moan on moan,
  And saw his death anigh, and said outright,
"I had all things, but love was worth them all!"
Then sped they for the Queen, yet ere the call

Reached her, he cried once more, "Too late! too late!"
  And at those words, before they led her in,
Came the sure dart of him that lay in wait.
  The Prince was dead: what goodness and what sin
Died with him were untold. At sunrise fell
Across the capital his solemn knell.

All respite it forbade, and joyance thence,
  To one for whom his passion till the last
Wrought in the dying Prince. Her wan suspense
  Thus ended, a great fear upon her passed.
"I was the cause!" she moaned from day to day,
"Now let me bear the penance as I may!"

So with her whole estate she sought and gained
  A refuge in a nunnery close at view,
And there for months withdrew her, and remained
  In tears and prayers. Anon a sickness grew
Upon her, and her face the ghost became
Of what it was, the same and not the same.

SO died the blameless Prince. The spacious land
Was smitten in his death, and such a wail
Arose, as when the midnight angel's hand
Was laid on Egypt. Gossips ceased their tale,
Or whispered of his goodness, and were mute;
No sound was heard of viol and of lute;

The streets were hung with black; the artisan
Forsook his forge; the artist dropped his brush;
The tradesmen closed their windows. Man with man
Struck hands together in the first deep hush
Of grief; or, where the dead Prince lay in state,
Spoke of his life, so blameless, pure, and great.

But when, within the dark cathedral vault,
They joined his ashes to the dust of kings,
No royal pomp was shown; for Death made halt
Above the palace yet, on dusky wings,
Waiting to gain the Queen, who still was prone
Along the couch where haply she had thrown,

At knowledge of the end, her stricken frame.
  With visage pale as in a mortal swound
She stayed, nor slept, nor wept, till, weeping, came
  The crown-prince and besought her to look round
And speak unto her children. Then she said:
"Hereto no grief has fallen on our head;

"Now all our earthly portion in one mass
  Is loosed against us with this single stroke!
Yet we are Queen, and still must live, — alas! —
  As he would have us." Even as she spoke
She wept, and mended thence, yet bore the face
Of one whose fate delays but for a space.

Thenceforth she worked and waited till the call
  Of Heaven should close the labor and the pause.
Months, seasons passed, yet evermore a pall
  Hung round the court. The sorrow and the cause
Were always with her; after things were tame
Beside the shadow of his deeds and fame.

Her palaces and parks seemed desolate;
  No joy was left in sky or street or field;
No age, she thought, would see the Prince's mate:
  What matchless hand his knightly sword could wield?
The world had lost, this royal widow said,
Its one bright jewel when the Prince was dead.

So that his fame might be enduring there
  For many a reign, and sacred through the land,
She gathered bronze and lazuli, and rare
  Swart marbles, while her cunning artists planned
A stately cenotaph, — and bade them place
Above its front the Prince's form and face,

Sculptured, as if in life. But the wan Queen,
  Watching the work herself, would somewhat lure
Her heart from plaining; till, behind a screen,
  The tomb was finished, glorious and pure,
Even like the Prince: and they proclaimed a day
When the Queen's hand should draw its veil away.

It chanced, the noon before, she bade them fetch
  Her equipage, and with her children rode
Beyond the city walls, across a stretch
  Of the green open country, where abode
Her subjects, happy in the field and grange,
And with their griefs, that took a meaner range,

Content. But as her joyless vision dwelt
  On beauty that so failed her wound to heal,
She marked the Abbey's ancient pile, and felt
  A longing at its chapel-shrine to kneel,
To pray, and think awhile on Heaven, — her one
Sole passion, now the Prince had thither gone.

She reached the gate, and through the vestibule
  The nuns, with reverence for the royal sorrow,
Led to the shrine, and left her there to school
  Her heart for that sad pageant of the morrow.
O, what deep sighs, what piteous tearful prayers,
What golden grief-blanched hair strewn unawares!

Anon her coming through the place was sped,
  And, when from that lone ecstasy she rose,
The saintly Abbess held her steps, and said:
  "God rests those, daughter, who in others' woes
Forget their own! In yonder corridor
A sister-sufferer lies, and will no more

"Pass through her door to catch the morning's breath:
  A worldling once, the chamberlain's young wife;
But now a pious novice, meet for death,
  She prays to see your face once more in life."
"She, too, is widowed," thought the Queen. Aloud
She answered, "I will visit her," and bowed

Her head, and, following, reached the room where lay
  One that had wronged her so; and shrank to see
That beauteous pallid face, so pined away,
  And the starved lips that murmured painfully,
"I have a secret none but she may hear."
At the Queen's sign, they two were left anear.

With that the dying rushed upon her speech,
  As one condemned, who gulps the poisoned wine
Nor pauses, lest to see it stand at reach
  Were crueller still. "Madam, I sought a sign,"
She cried, "to know if God would have me make
Confession, and to you! now let me take

"This meeting as the sign, and speak, and die!"
  "Child," said the Queen, "your years are yet too few.
See how I live, — and yet what sorrows lie
  About my heart." — "I know, — the world spake true!
You too have loved him; ay, he seems to stand
Between us! Queen, you had the Prince's hand,

"But not his love!" Across the good Queen's brow
  A flame of anger reddened, as when one
Meets unprepared a swift and ruthless blow,
  But instant paled to pity, as she thought,
"She wanders: 't is the fever at her brain!"
And looked her thought. The other cried again:

"Yes! I am ill of body and soul indeed,
  Yet this was as I say. O, not for me
Pity, from you who wear the widow's weed,
  Unknowing!"—"Woman, whose could that love be,
If not all mine?" The other, with a moan,
Rose in her bed: the pillow, backward thrown,

Was darkened with the torrent of her hair.
  "'T was hers," she wailed,—"'t was hers who loved
    him best."
Then tore apart her night-robe, and laid bare
  Her flesh, and lo! against her poor white breast
Close round her gloomed a shift of blackest serge,
Fearful, concealed!—"I might not sing his dirge,"

She said, "nor moan aloud and bring him shame,
  Nor haunt his tomb and cling about the grate,
But this I fashioned when the tidings came
  That he was dead and I must expiate,
Being left, our double sin!" In the Queen's heart
The tiger—that is prisoned at life's start

In mortals, though perchance it never wakes
  From its mute sleep — began to rouse and crawl.
Her lips grew white, and on her nostrils flakes
  Of wrath and loathing stood. "What, now, is all
This wicked drivel?" she cried; "how dare they bring
The Queen to listen to so foul a thing?"

"Queen! I speak truth,—the truth, I say! He fed
  Upon these lips, — this hair he loved to praise!
I held within these arms his bright fair head
  Pressed close, ah, close! — Our lifetimes were the days
We met, — the rest a void!" — "Thou spectral Sin,
Be silent! or, if such a thing hath been, —

"If this be not thy frenzy, — quick, the proof,
  Before I score the lie thy lips amid!"
She spoke so dread the other crouched aloof,
  Panting, but with gaunt hands somewhere undid
A knot within her hair, and thence she took
The signet-ring and passed it. The Queen's look

Fell on it, and that moment the strong stay,
  Which held her from the instinct of her wrong,
Broke, and therewith the whole device gave way,
  The grand ideal she had watched so long:
As if a tower should fall, and on the plain
Only a scathed and broken pile remain.

But in its stead she would not measure yet
  The counter-chance, nor deem this sole attaint
Made the Prince less than one in whom 't was set
  To prove him man. "I held him as a saint,"
She thought, "no other: — of all men alone
My blameless one! Too high my faith had flown:

"So be it!" With a sudden bitter scorn
  She said: "You were his plaything, then! the food
Wherewith he dulled what appetite is born,
  Of the gross kind, in men. His nobler mood
You knew not! How, shall I, — the fountain life
Of yonder children, — his embosomed wife

"Through all these years, — shall I, his Queen, for this
Sin-smitten harlot's gage of an hour's shame,
Misdoubt him?" — "Yes, I was his harlot, — yes,
God help me! and had worn the loathly name
Before the world, to have him in that guise!"
"Thou strumpet! wilt thou have me of his prize

"Rob Satan?" cried the Queen, and one step moved.
"Queen, if you loved him, save me from your bane,
As something that was dear to him you loved!"
Then from beneath her serge she took the chain
Which, long ago in that lone wood, the Prince
Hung round her, — she had never loosed it since, —

And gave therewith the face which, in its years
Of youthful, sunniest grace, a limner drew;
And unsigned letters, darkened with her tears,
Writ in the hand that hapless sovereign knew
Too well; — then told the whole, strange, secret tale,
As if with Heaven that penance could avail,

Or with the Queen, who heard as idols list
  The mad priest's cry, nor changed her place nor moaned,
But, clutching those mute tokens of each tryst,
  Hid them about her. But the other groaned:
"The picture, — let me see it ere I die, —
Then take them all! once, only!"— At that cry

The Queen strode forward with an awful stride,
  And seized the dying one, and bore her down,
And rose her height, and said, "Thou shouldst have died
  Ere telling this, nor I have worn a crown
To hear it told. I am of God accurst!
Of all his hated, may he smite thee first!"

With that wild speech she fled, nor looked behind,
  Hasting to get her from that fearful room,
Past the meek nuns in wait. These did not find
  The sick one's eyes — set staring through the gloom,
While her hands fumbled at her heart, and Death
Made her limbs quake, and combated her breath —

More dreadful than the Queen's look, as she thence
  Made through the court, and reached her own array
She knew not how, and clamored, "Bear me hence!"
  And, even as her chariot moved away,
High o'er the Abbey heard the minster toll
Its doleful bell, as for a passing soul.

Though midst her guardsmen, as they speeded back,
  The wont of royalty maintained her still,
Where grief had been were ruin now and rack!
  The firm earth reeled about, nor could her will
Make it seem stable, while her soul went through
Her wedded years in desperate review;

The air seemed full of lies; the realm, unsound;
  Her courtiers, knaves; her maidens, good and fair,
Most shameless bawds; her children clung around
  Like asps, to sting her; from the kingdom's heir,
Shuddering, she turned her face, — his features took
A shining horror from his father's look.

Along her city streets the thrifty crowd,
  As the Queen passed, their loving reverence made.
"'T is false! they love me not!" she cried aloud;
  So flung her from her chariot, and forbade
All words, but waved her ladies back, and gained
Her inmost room, and by herself remained.

"We have been alone these years, and knew it not,"
  She said; "now let us on the knowledge thrive!"
So closed the doors, and all things else forgot
  Than her own misery. "I cannot live
And bear this death," she said, "nor die, the more
To meet him, — and that woman gone before!"

Thus with herself she writhed, while midnight gloomed,
  As lone as any outcast of us all;
And once, without a purpose, as the doomed
  Stare round and count the shadows on the wall,
Unclasped a poet's book which near her lay,
And turned its pages in that witless way,

And read the song some wise sad man had made
  With bitter frost about his doubting heart.
"What is this life," it plained, "what masquerade
  Of which ye all are witnesses and part?
'T is but a foolish, smiling face to wear
Above your mortal sorrow, chill despair;

"To mock your comrades and yourselves with mirth
  That feeds the care ye cannot drive away;
To vaunt of health, yet hide beneath the girth
  Impuissance, fell sickness, slow decay;
To cloak defeat, and with the rich, the great,
Applaud their fairer fortunes as their mate;

"To brave the sudden woe, the secret loss,
  Though but to-morrow brings the open shame;
To pay the tribute of your caste, and toss
  Your last to him that 's richer save in name;
To judge your peers, and give the doleful meed
To crime that 's white beside your hidden deed;

"To whisper love, where of true love is none, —
Desire, where lust is dead; to live unchaste,
And wear the priestly cincture; — last, to own,
When the morn's dream is gone and noontide waste,
Some fate still kept ye from your purpose sweet,
Down strange, circuitous paths it drew your feet!"

Thus far she read, and, "Let me read no more,"
She clamored, "since the scales have left mine eyes
And freed the dreadful gift I lacked before!
We are but puppets, in whatever guise
They clothe us, to whatever tune we move;
Albeit we prate of duty, dream of love.

"Let me, too, play the common part, and wean
My life from hope, and look beneath the mask
To learn the masker! I, who was a Queen,
And like a hireling thought to 'scape my task!
For some few seasons left this heart is schooled:
Yet, — had it been a little longer fooled, —

"O God!" And from her seat she bowed her down.
  The gentle sovereign of that spacious land
Lay prone beneath the bawble of her crown,
  Nor heard all night her whispering ladies stand
Outside the portal. Greatly, in the morn,
They marvelled at her visage wan and worn.

BUT when the sun was high, the populace
  By every gateway filled the roads, and sought
The martial plain, within whose central space
  That wonder of the Prince's tomb was wrought.
Thereto from out the nearer land there passed
The mingled folk, an eager throng and vast;

Knights, commons, men and women, young and old,
  The present and the promise of the realm.
Anon the coming of the Queen was told,
  And mounted guards, with sable plumes at helm,
Made through the middle, like a reaper's swath,
A straight, wide roadway for the sovereign's path.

Then rose the murmurous sound of her advance,
  And, with the crown-prince, and her other brood
Led close behind, she came. Her countenance
  Moved not to right nor left, until she stood
Before the tomb; yet those, who took the breath
That clothed her progress, felt a waft of death.

O noble martyr! queenliest intent!
  Strong human soul, that holds to pride through all!
Ah me! with what fierce heavings in them pent
  The brave complete their work, whate'er befall!
Upon her front the people only read
Pale grief that clung forever to the dead.

How should they know she trod the royal stand,
  And took within her hold the silken line,
As, while the headsman waits, one lays her hand
  Upon the scarf that slays her by a sign?
With one great pang she drew the veil, and lo!
The work was dazzling in the noonday glow.

There shone the Prince's image, golden, high,
  Installed forever in the people's sight.
"Alas!" they cried, "too good, too fair to die!"
  But at the foot the Queen had bid them write
Her consort's goodness, and his glory-roll,
Yet knew not they had carved upon the scroll

That last assurance of his stainless heart, —
  For such they deemed his words who heard them fall:
"*Of all great things this Prince achieved his part,*
  Yet wedded Love to him was worth them all."
Thus read the Queen: till now, her injured soul
Of its forlornness had not felt the whole.

Now all her heart was broken. There she fell,
  And to the skies her lofty spirit fled.
The wrong of those mute words had smitten well.
  A cry went up: "The Queen! the Queen is dead!
O regal heart that would not reign alone!
O fatal sorrow! O the empty throne!"

Her people made her beauteous relics room
  Within the chamber where her consort slept.
There rest they side by side. Around the tomb
  A thousand matrons solemn vigil kept.
Long ages told the story of her reign,
And sang the nuptial love that had no stain.

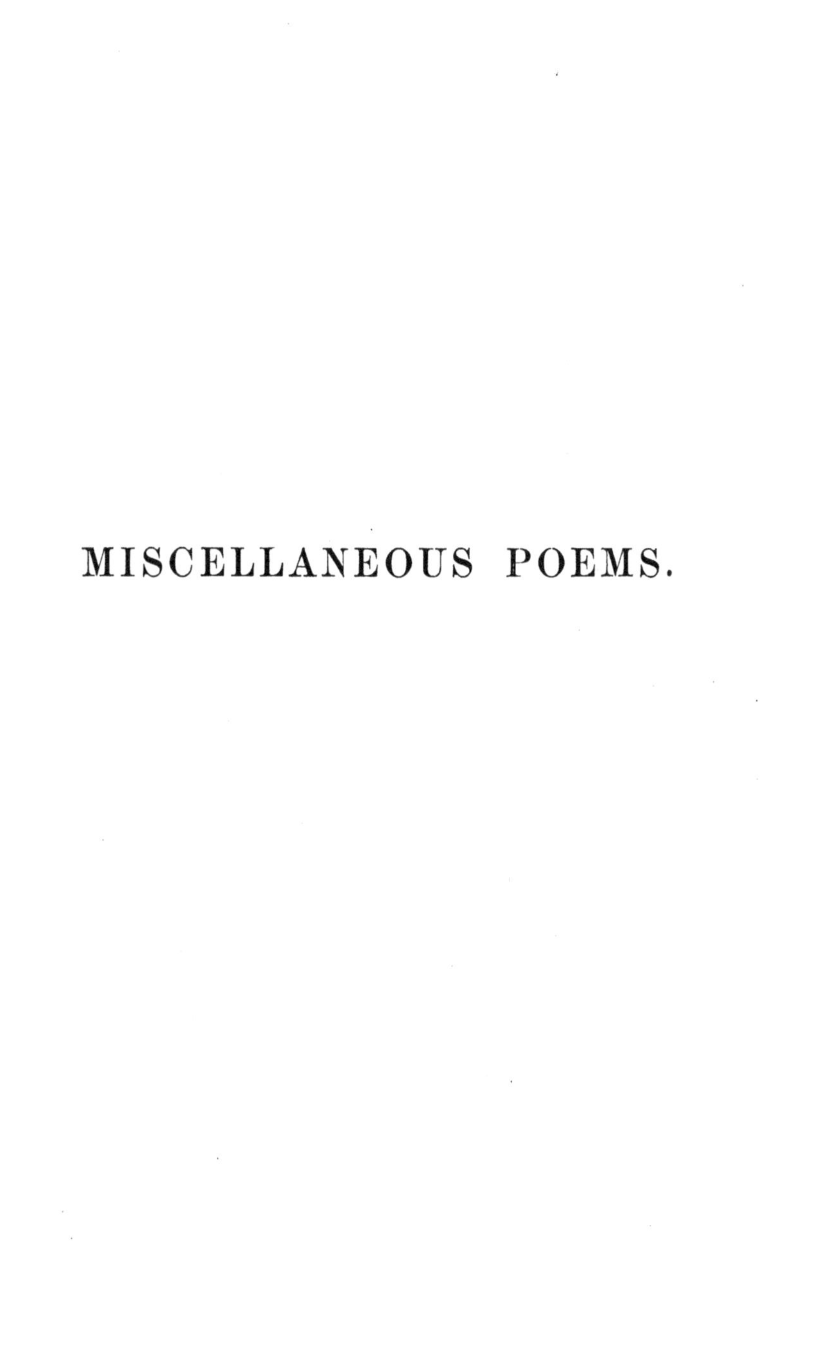

MISCELLANEOUS POEMS.

I.

SONGS AND STUDIES.

SONGS AND STUDIES.

SURF.

SPLENDORS of morning the billow-crests brighten,
Lighting and luring them on to the land, —
Far-away waves where the wan vessels whiten,
Blue rollers breaking in surf where we stand.
Curved like the necks of a legion of horses,
Each with his froth-gilded mane flowing free,
Hither they speed in perpetual courses,
Bearing thy riches, O beautiful sea!

Strong with the striving of yesterday's surges,
Lashed by the wanton winds leagues from the shore,
Each, driven fast by its follower, urges
Fearlessly those that are fleeting before;

How they leap over the ridges we walk on,
  Flinging us gifts from the depths of the sea, —
Silvery fish for the foam-haunting falcon,
  Palm-weed and pearls for my darling and me!

Light falls her foot where the rift follows after,
  Finer her hair than your feathery spray,
Sweeter her voice than your infinite laughter, —
  Hist! ye wild couriers, list to my lay!
Deep in the chambers of grottoes auroral
  Morn laves her jewels and bends her red knee:
Thence to my dear one your amber and coral
  Bring for her dowry, O beautiful sea!

TOUJOURS AMOUR.

PRITHEE tell me, Dimple-Chin,
At what age does Love begin?
Your blue eyes have scarcely seen
Summers three, my fairy queen,
But a miracle of sweets,
Soft approaches, sly retreats,
Show the little archer there,
Hidden in your pretty hair;
When didst learn a heart to win?
Prithee tell me, Dimple Chin!

"Oh!" the rosy lips reply,
"I can't tell you if I try.
'T is so long I can't remember:
Ask some younger lass than I!

Tell, O tell me, Grizzled-Face,
Do your heart and head keep pace?

When does hoary Love expire,
When do frosts put out the fire?
Can its embers burn below
All that chill December snow?
Care you still soft hands to press,
Bonny heads to smooth and bless?
When does Love give up the chase?
Tell, O tell me, Grizzled-Face!

"Ah!" the wise old lips reply,
"Youth may pass and strength may die;
But of Love I can't foretoken:
Ask some older sage than I!"

LAURA, MY DARLING.

LAURA, my darling, the roses have blushed
At the kiss of the dew, and our chamber is hushed ;
Our murmuring babe to your bosom has clung,
And hears in his slumber the song that you sung ;
I watch you asleep with your arms round him thrown,
Your links of dark tresses wound in with his own,
And the wife is as dear as the gentle young bride
Of the hour when you first, darling, came to my side.

Laura, my darling, our sail down the stream
Of Youth's summers and winters has been like a dream ;
Years have but rounded your womanly grace,
And added their spell to the light of your face ;
Your soul is the same as though part were not given
To the two, like yourself, sent to bless me from heaven, —
Dear lives, springing forth from the life of my life,
To make you more near, darling, mother and wife !

Laura, my darling, there 's hazel-eyed Fred,
Asleep in his own tiny cot by the bed,
And little King Arthur, whose curls have the art
Of winding their tendrils so close round my heart, —
Yet fairer than either, and dearer than both,
Is the true one who gave me in girlhood her troth:
For we, when we mated for evil and good, —
What were we, darling, but babes in the wood?

Laura, my darling, the years which have flown
Brought few of the prizes I pledged to my own.
I said that no sorrow should roughen her way, —
Her life should be cloudless, a long summer's day.
Shadow and sunshine, thistles and flowers,
Which of the two, darling, most have been ours?
Yet to-night, by the smile on your lips, I can see
You are dreaming of me, darling, dreaming of me

Laura, my darling, the stars, that we knew
In our youth, are still shining as tender and true:
The midnight is sounding its slumberous bell,
And I come to the one who has loved me so well.

Wake, darling, wake, for my vigil is done:
What shall dissever our lives which are one?
Say, while the rose listens under her breath,
"Naught until death, darling, naught until death!"

THE TRYST.

SLEEPING, I dreamed that thou wast mine,
In some ambrosial lovers' shrine.
My lips against thy lips were pressed,
And all our passion was confessed;
So near and dear my darling seemed,
I knew not that I only dreamed.

Waking, this mid and moonlit night,
I clasp thee close by lover's right.
Thou fearest not my warm embrace,
And yet, so like the dream thy face
And kisses, I but half partake
The joy, and know not if I wake.

VIOLET EYES.

ONE can never quite forget
Eyes like yours, May Margaret,
Eyes of dewy violet!
Nothing like them, Margaret,
Save the blossoms newly born
Of the May and of the Morn.

Oft my memory wanders back
To those burning eyes and black,
Whose heat-lightnings once could move
Me to passion, not to love;
Longer in my heart of hearts
Linger those disguisèd arts,
Which, betimes, a hazel pair
Used upon me unaware;
And the wise and tender gray, —
Eyes wherewith a saint might pray, —

Speak of pledges that endure
And of faith and vigils pure;
But for him who fain would know
All the fire the first can show,
All the art, or friendship fast,
Of the second and the last, —
And would gain a subtler worth,
Part of Heaven, part of Earth, —
He these mingled rays can find
In but one immortal kind:
In those eyes of violet,
In *your* eyes, May Margaret!

THE DOORSTEP.

THE conference-meeting through at last,
  We boys around the vestry waited
To see the girls come tripping past
  Like snow-birds willing to be mated.

Not braver he that leaps the wall
  By level musket-flashes litten,
Than I, who stepped before them all
  Who longed to see me get the mitten.

But no, she blushed and took my arm!
  We let the old folks have the highway,
And started toward the Maple Farm
  Along a kind of lovers' by-way.

I can't remember what we said,
  'T was nothing worth a song or story;
Yet that rude path by which we sped
  Seemed all transformed and in a glory.

The snow was crisp beneath our feet,
  The moon was full, the fields were gleaming;
By hood and tippet sheltered sweet,
  Her face with youth and health was beaming.

The little hand outside her muff, —
  O sculptor, if you could but mould it!
So lightly touched my jacket-cuff,
  To keep it warm I had to hold it.

To have her with me there alone,—
  'T was love and fear and triumph blended.
At last we reached the foot-worn stone
  Where that delicious journey ended.

The old folks, too, were almost home;
  Her dimpled hand the latches fingered,
We heard the voices nearer come,
  Yet on the doorstep still we lingered.

She shook her ringlets from her hood
  And with a "Thank you, Ned," dissembled,
But yet I knew she understood
  With what a daring wish I trembled.

A cloud passed kindly overhead,
  The moon was slyly peeping through it,
Yet hid its face, as if it said,
  "Come, now or never! do it! *do it!*"

My lips till then had only known
  The kiss of mother and of sister,
But somehow, full upon her own
  Sweet, rosy, darling mouth, — I kissed her!

Perhaps 't was boyish love, yet still,
  O listless woman, weary lover!
To feel once more that fresh, wild thrill
  I 'd give, — but who can live youth over?

ILIUM FUIT.

ONE by one they died, —
Last of all their race;
Nothing left but pride,
Lace, and buckled hose.
Their quietus made,
On their dwelling-place
Ruthless hands are laid:
Down the old house goes!

See the ancient manse
Meet its fate at last!
Time, in his advance,
Age nor honor knows;
Axe and broadaxe fall,
Lopping off the Past:
Hit with bar and maul,
Down the old house goes!

Sevenscore years it stood:
  Yes, they built it well,
Though they built of wood,
    When that house arose.
For its cross-beams square
  Oak and walnut fell;
Little worse for wear,
    Down the old house goes!

Rending board and plank,
  Men with crow-bars ply,
Opening fissures dank,
    Striking deadly blows.
From the gabled roof
  How the shingles fly!
Keep you here aloof, —
    Down the old house goes!

Holding still its place,
  There the chimney stands,
Stanch from top to base,
    Frowning on its foes.

Heave apart the stones,
  Burst its iron bands!
How it shakes and groans!
    Down the old house goes!

Round the mantel-piece
  Glisten Scripture tiles;
Henceforth they shall cease
    Painting Egypt's woes,
Painting David's fight,
  Fair Bathsheba's smiles,
Blinded Samson's might, —
    Down the old house goes!

On these oaken floors
  High-shoed ladies trod;
Through those panelled doors
    Trailed their furbelows:
Long their day has ceased;
  Now, beneath the sod,
With the worms they feast, —
    Down the old house goes!

Many a bride has stood
  In yon spacious room;
Here her hand was wooed
    Underneath the rose;
O'er that sill the dead
  Reached the family-tomb:
All, that were, have fled,—
    Down the old house goes!

Once, in yonder hall,
  Washington, they say,
Led the New-Year's ball,
    Stateliest of beaux.
O that minuet,
  Maids and matrons gay!
Are there such sights yet?
    Down the old house goes!

British troopers came
  Ere another year,
With their coats aflame,
    Mincing on their toes;

Daughters of the house
  Gave them haughty cheer,
Laughed to scorn their vows, —
    Down the old house goes!

Doorway high the box
  In the grass-plot spreads;
It has borne its locks
    Through a thousand snows;
In an evil day,
  From those garden-beds
Now 't is hacked away, —
    Down the old house goes!

Lo! the sycamores,
  Scathed and scrawny mates,
At the mansion doors
    Shiver, full of woes;
With its life they grew,
  Guarded well its gates;
Now their task is through, —
    Down the old house goes!

On this honored site
  Modern trade will build, —
What unseemly fright
    Heaven only knows!
Something peaked and high,
  Smacking of the guild:
Let us heave a sigh, —
    Down the old house goes

COUNTRY SLEIGHING.

A NEW SONG TO AN OLD TUNE.

IN January, when down the dairy
  The cream and clabber freeze,
When snow-drifts cover the fences over,
  We farmers take our ease.
At night we rig the team,
  And bring the cutter out;
Then fill it, fill it, fill it, fill it,
  And heap the furs about.

Here friends and cousins dash up by dozens,
  And sleighs at least a score;
There John and Molly, behind, are jolly, —
  Nell rides with me, before.
All down the village street
  We range us in a row:
Now jingle, jingle, jingle, jingle,
  And over the crispy snow!

The windows glisten, the old folks listen
  To hear the sleigh-bells pass ;
The fields grow whiter, the stars are brighter,
  The road is smooth as glass.
Our muffled faces burn,
  The clear north-wind blows cold,
The girls all nestle, nestle, nestle,
  Each in her lover's hold.

Through bridge and gateway we're shooting straightway,
  Their tollman was too slow !
He 'll listen after our song and laughter
  As over the hill we go.
The girls cry, "Fie ! for shame !"
  Their cheeks and lips are red,
And so, with kisses, kisses, kisses,
  They take the toll instead.

Still follow, follow ! across the hollow
  The tavern fronts the road.
Whoa, now ! all steady ! the host is ready, —
  He knows the country mode !

The irons are in the fire,
  The hissing flip is got;
So pour and sip it, sip it, sip it,
  And sip it while 't is hot.

Push back the tables, and from the stables
  Bring Tom, the fiddler, in;
All take your places, and make your graces,
  And let the dance begin.
The girls are beating time
  To hear the music sound;
Now foot it, foot it, foot it, foot it,
  And swing your partners round.

Last couple toward the left! all forward!
  Cotillons through, let 's wheel:
First tune the fiddle, then down the middle
  In old Virginia Reel.
Play Money Musk to close,
  Then take the "long chassé,"
While in to supper, supper, supper,
  The landlord leads the way.

The bells are ringing, the ostlers bringing
  The cutters up anew ;
The beasts are neighing ; too long we 're staying,
  The night is half-way through.
Wrap close the buffalo-robes,
  We 're all aboard once more ;
Now jingle, jingle, jingle, jingle,
  Away from the tavern-door.

So follow, follow, by hill and hollow,
  And swiftly homeward glide.
What midnight splendor! how warm and tender
  The maiden by your side!
The sleighs drop far apart,
  Her words are soft and low ;
Now, if you love her, love her, love her,
  'T is safe to tell her so.

PAN IN WALL STREET.

A. D. 1867.

JUST where the Treasury's marble front
  Looks over Wall Street's mingled nations, —
Where Jews and Gentiles most are wont
  To throng for trade and last quotations, —
Where, hour by hour, the rates of gold
  Outrival, in the ears of people,
The quarter-chimes, serenely tolled
  From Trinity's undaunted steeple ; —

Even there I heard a strange, wild strain
  Sound high above the modern clamor,
Above the cries of greed and gain,
  The curbstone war, the auction's hammer, —
And swift, on Music's misty ways,
  It led, from all this strife for millions,
To ancient, sweet-do-nothing days
  Among the kirtle-robed Sicilians.

And as it stilled the multitude,
  And yet more joyous rose, and shriller,
I saw the minstrel, where he stood
  At ease against a Doric pillar:
One hand a droning organ played,
  The other held a Pan's-pipe (fashioned
Like those of old) to lips that made
  The reeds give out that strain impassioned.

'T was Pan himself had wandered here
  A-strolling through this sordid city,
And piping to the civic ear
  The prelude of some pastoral ditty!
The demigod had crossed the seas, —
  From haunts of shepherd, nymph, and satyr
And Syracusan times, — to these
  Far shores and twenty centuries later.

A ragged cap was on his head:
  But — hidden thus — there was no doubting
That, all with crispy locks o'erspread,
  His gnarlèd horns were somewhere sprouting;

His club-feet, cased in rusty shoes,
Were crossed, as on some frieze you see them,
And trousers, patched of divers hues,
Concealed his crooked shanks beneath them.

He filled the quivering reeds with sound,
And o'er his mouth their changes shifted,
And with his goat's-eyes looked around
Where'er the passing current drifted;
And soon, as on Trinacrian hills
The nymphs and herdsmen ran to hear him,
Even now the tradesmen from their tills,
With clerks and porters, crowded near him.

The bulls and bears together drew
From Jauncey Court and New Street Alley,
As erst, if pastorals be true,
Came beasts from every wooded valley;
The random passers stayed to list, —
A boxer Ægon, rough and merry, —
A Broadway Daphnis, on his tryst
With Nais at the Brooklyn Ferry.

A one-eyed Cyclops halted long
  In tattered cloak of army pattern,
And Galatea joined the throng, —
  A blowsy, apple-vending slattern;
While old Silenus staggered out
  From some new-fangled lunch-house handy,
And bade the piper, with a shout,
  To strike up Yankee Doodle Dandy!

A newsboy and a peanut-girl
  Like little Fauns began to caper:
His hair was all in tangled curl,
  Her tawny legs were bare and taper;
And still the gathering larger grew,
  And gave its pence and crowded nigher,
While aye the shepherd-minstrel blew
  His pipe, and struck the gamut higher.

O heart of Nature, beating still
  With throbs her vernal passion taught her, —
Even here, as on the vine-clad hill,
  Or by the Arethusan water!

New forms may fold the speech, new lands
  Arise within these ocean-portals,
But Music waves eternal wands, —
  Enchantress of the souls of mortals!

So thought I, — but among us trod
  A man in blue, with legal baton,
And scoffed the vagrant demigod,
  And pushed him from the step I sat on.
Doubting I mused upon the cry,
  "Great Pan is dead!" — and all the people
Went on their ways: — and clear and high
  The quarter sounded from the steeple.

ANONYMA.

HER CONFESSION.

IF I had been a rich man's girl,
With my tawny hair, and this wanton art
Of lifting my eyes in the evening whirl
And looking into another's heart;
Had love been mine at birth, and friends
Caressing and guarding me night and day,
With doctors to watch my finger-ends,
And a parson to teach me how to pray;

If I had been reared as others have, —
With but a tithe of these looks, which came
From my reckless mother, now in her grave,
And the father who grudged me even his name, —
Why, I should have station and tender care,
Should ruin men in the high-bred way,
Passionless, smiling at their despair,
And marrying where my vantage lay.

As it is, I must have love and dress,
  Jewelled trinkets, and costly food,
For I was born for plenteousness,
  Music and flowers, and all things good ;
To that same father I owe some thanks,
  Seeing, at least, that blood will tell,
And keep me ever above the ranks
  Of those who wallow where they fell

True, there are weary, weary days
  In the great hotel where I make my lair,
Where I meet the men with their brutal praise,
  Or answer the women, stare for stare.
'T is an even fight, and I 'll carry it through, —
  Pit them against me, great and small :
I grant no quarter, nor would I sue
  For grace to the softest of them all

I cannot remember half the men
  Whose sin has tangled them in my toils, —
All are alike before me then,
  Part of my easily conquered spoils :

Tall or short, and dark or fair,
  Rich or famous, haughty or fond,
There are few, I find, who will not forswear
  The lover's oath and the wedding bond.

Fools! what is it that drives them on
  With their perjured lips on poison fed;
Vain of themselves, and cruel as stone,
  How should they be so cheaply led?
Surely they know me as I am, —
  Only a cuckoo, at the best,
Watching, careless of hate and shame,
  To crouch myself in another's nest.

But the women, — how they flutter and flout,
  The stupid, terribly virtuous wives,
If I but chance to move about
  Or enter within their bustling hives!
Buz! buz! in the scandalous gatherings,
  When a strange queen lights amid their throng,
And their tongues have a thousand angry stings
  To send her travelling, right or wrong.

Well, the earth is wide and open to all,
  And money and men are everywhere,
And, as I roam, 't will ill befall
  If I do not gain my lawful share:
One drops off, but another will come
  With as light a head and heavy a purse;
So long as I have the world for a home,
  I 'll take my fortune, better or worse!

SPOKEN AT SEA.

THE LOG-BOOK OF THE STEAMSHIP VIRGINIA.

TWELVE hundred miles and more
From the stormy English shore,
All aright, the seventh night,
On her course our vessel bore.
Her lantern shone ahead,
And the green lamp and the red
To starboard and to larboard
Shot their light.

Close on the midnight call
What a mist began to fall,
And to hide the ocean wide,
And to wrap us in a pall!
Beneath its folds we past:
Hidden were shroud and mast,
And faces, in near places
Side by side.

Sudden there also fell
A summons like a knell:
  Every ear the words could hear, —
Whence spoken, who could tell?
"What ship is this? where bound?"
Gods, what a dismal sound!
  A stranger, and in danger,
    Sailing near.

"The Virginia, on her route
From the Mersey, seven days out;
  Fore and aft, our trusty craft
Carries a thousand souls, about."
"All these souls may travel still,
Westward bound, if so they will;
  Bodies rather, I would gather!"
    Loud he laughed.

"Who is 't that hails so rude,
And for what this idle mood?
  Words like these, on midnight seas,
Bode no friend nor fortune good!"

"Care not to know my name,
But whence I lastly came,
  At leisure, for my pleasure,
    Ask the breeze.

"To the people of your port
Bear a message of this sort:
  Say, I haste unto the West,
A sharer of their sport.
Let them sweep the houses clean:
Their fathers did, I ween,
  When hearing of my nearing
    As a guest!

"As by Halifax ye sail
And the steamship England hail,
  Of me, then, bespeak her men;
She took my latest mail, —
'T was somewhere near this spot:
Doubtless they 've not forgot.
  Remind them (if you find them!)
    Once again.

"Yet that you all may know
Who is 't that hailed you so,
(Slow he saith, and under breath,)
I leave my sign below!"
Then from our crowded hold
A dreadful cry uprolled,
Unbroken, and the token, —
It was Death.

THE DUKE'S EXEQUY.

ARRAS, A. D. 1404.

CLOTHED in sable, crowned with gold,
All his wars and councils ended,
Philip lay, surnamed The Bold:
Passing-bell his quittance tolled,
And the chant of priests ascended.

Mailéd knights and archers stand,
Thronging in the church of Arras;
Nevermore at his command
Shall they scour the Netherland,
Nevermore the outlaws harass;

Naught is left of his array
Save a barren territory;
Forty years of generous sway
Sped his princely hoards away,
Bartered all his gold for glory.

Forth steps Flemish Margaret then,
Striding toward the silent ashes;
And the eyes of arméd men
Fill with startled wonder, when
On the bier her girdle clashes!

Swift she drew it from her waist,
And the purse and keys it carried
On the ducal coffin placed;
Then with proud demeanor faced
Sword and shield of him she married.

"No encumbrance of the dead
Must the living clog forever;
From thy debts and dues," she said,
"From the liens of thy bed,
We this day our line dissever.

"From thy hand we gain release,
Know all present by this token!
Let the dead repose in peace,
Let the claims upon us cease
When the ties that bound are broken.

"Philip, we have loved thee long,
But, in years of future splendor,
Burgundy shall count among
Bravest deeds of tale and song
This, our widowhood's surrender."

Back the stately Duchess turned,
While the priests and friars chanted,
And the swinging incense burned:
Thus by feudal rite was earned
Greatness for a race undaunted.

THE HILLSIDE DOOR.

SOMETIMES within my hand
A Spirit puts the silver key
Of Fairyland:
From the dark, barren heath he beckons me,
Till by that hidden hillside door,
Where bards have passed before,
I seem to stand.

The portal opens wide:
In, through the wondrous, lighted halls,
Voiceless I glide
Where tinkling music magically falls,
And fair in fountained gardens move
The heroes, blest with love
And glorified.

Then by the meadows green,
Down winding walks of elf and fay,
I pass unseen:
There rest the valiant chieftains wreathed with bay;
Here maidens to their lovers cling,
And happy minstrels sing,
Praising their queen.

For where yon pillars are,
And birds with tuneful voices call,
There shines a star, —
The crown she wears, the Fairy Queen of all!
Led to that inmost, wooded haunt
By maidens ministrant,
I halt afar.

O joy! she sees me stand
Doubting, and calls me near her throne,
And waves her wand,
As in my dreams, and smiles on me alone.
O royal beauty, proud and sweet!
I bow me at her feet
To kiss that hand:

Ah woe! ah, fate malign!
By what a rude, revengeful gust,
From that fair shrine
Which holds my sovran mistress I am thrust!
Then comes a mocking voice's taunt,
Crying, *Thou fool, avaunt!*
She is not thine!

And I am backward borne
By unseen awful hands, and cast,
In utter scorn,
Forth from that brightness to the midnight blast:
Not mine the minstrel-lover's wreath,
But the dark, barren heath,
And heart forlorn.

AT TWILIGHT.

THE sunset darkens in the west,
 The sea-gulls haunt the bay,
And far and high the swallows fly
 To watch the dying day.
Now where is she that once with me
 The rippling waves would list?
And O for the song I loved so long,
 And the darling lips I kist!

Yon twinkling sail may whiter gleam
 Than falcon's snowy wing,
Her lances far the evening-star
 Beyond the waves may fling;
Float on, ah float, enchanted boat,
 Bear true hearts o'er the main,
But I shall guide thy helm no more,
 Nor whisper love again!

II.

POEMS OF NATURE.

POEMS OF NATURE.

WOODS AND WATERS.

"O ye valleys! O ye mountains!
O ye groves and crystal fountains!
How I love at liberty,
By turns, to come and visit ye!"

COME, let us burst the cerements and the shroud,
And with the livelong year renew our breath,
Far from the darkness of the city's cloud
Which hangs above us like the pall of Death:
Haste, let us leave the shadow of his wings!
Off from our cares, a stolen, happy time!
Come where the skies are blue, the uplands green;
For hark! the robin sings
Even here, blithe herald, his auroral rhyme,
Foretelling joy, and June his sovereign queen.

See, in our paved courts her missal scroll
  Is dropped astealth, and every verdant line,
Emblazoned round with Summer's aureole,
  Pictures to eager eyes, like thine and mine,
Her trees new-leaved and hillsides far away.
  Ransom has come: out from this vaulted town,
    Poor prisoners of a giant old and blind,
      Into the breezy day,
  Fleeing the sights and sounds that wear us down,
    And in the fields our ancient solace find!

Again I hunger for the living wood,
  The laurelled crags, the hemlocks hanging wide,
The rushing stream that will not be withstood,
  Bound forward to wed him with the river's tide:
O what wild leaps through many a fettered pass,
  Through knotted ambuscade of root and rock,
    How white the plunge, how dark the cloven pool!
      Then to rich meadow-grass,
  And pastures fed by tinkling herd and flock,
    Till the wide stream receives its waters cool.

Again I long for lakes that lie between
  High mountains, fringed about with virgin firs,
Where hand of man has never rudely been,
  Nor plashing wheel the limpid water stirs;
There let us twain begin the world again
  Like those of old, — while tree, and trout, and deer,
    Unto their kindred beings draw our own,
      Till more than haunts of men,
  Than place and pelf, more welcome these appear,
    And better worth sheer life than we had known.

Thither, ay, thither flee, O dearest friend,
  From walls wherein we grow so wan and old!
The liberal Earth will still her lovers lend
  Water of life and storied sands of gold;
Though of her perfect form thou hast secured
  Thy will, some charm shall aye thine hold defy,
    And day by day thy passion yet shall grow,
      Even as a bridegroom, lured
  By the unravished secret of her eye,
    Reads the bride's soul, yet never all can know.

And when from her embrace again thou 'rt torn,
  (Though well for her the world were thrown away!)
At thine old tasks thou 'lt not be quite forlorn,
  Remembering where is peace; and thou shalt say,
"I know where beauty has not felt the curse, —
  Where, though I age, all round me is so young
    That in its youth my soul's youth mirrored seems;
      Yes, in their rippling verse,
  For all our toil, they have not falsely sung
    Who said there still was rest beyond our dreams."

TO B. T.

WITH A COPY OF THE ILIAD.

BAYARD, awaken not this music strong,
While round thy home the indolent sweet breeze
Floats lightly as the summer breath of seas
O'er which Ulysses heard the Sirens' song.
Dreams of low-lying isles to June belong,
And Circe holds us in her haunts of ease:
But later, when these high ancestral trees
Are sere, and such melodious languors wrong
The reddening strength of the autumnal year,
Yield to heroic words thy ear and eye; —
Intent on these broad pages thou shalt hear
The trumpets' blare, the Argive battle-cry,
And see Achilles hurl his hurtling spear,
And mark the Trojan arrows make reply!

THE MOUNTAIN.

TWO thousand feet in air it stands
  Betwixt the bright and shaded lands,
Above the regions it divides
And borders with its furrowed sides.
The seaward valley laughs with light
Till the round sun o'erhangs this height;
But then the shadow of the crest
No more the plains that lengthen west
Enshrouds, yet slowly, surely creeps
Eastward, until the coolness steeps
A darkling league of tilth and wold,
And chills the flocks that seek their fold.

Not like those ancient summits lone,
Mont Blanc, on his eternal throne,—
The city-gemmed Peruvian peak,—
The sunset portals landsmen seek,

Whose train, to reach the Golden Land,
Crawls slow and pathless through the sand, —
Or that, whose ice-lit beacon guides
The mariner on tropic tides,
And flames across the Gulf afar,
A torch by day, by night a star, —
Not thus, to cleave the outer skies,
Does my serener mountain rise,
Nor aye forget its gentle birth
Upon the dewy, pastoral earth.

But ever, in the noonday light,
Are scenes whereof I love the sight, —
Broad pictures of the lower world
Beneath my gladdened eyes unfurled.
Irradiate distances reveal
Fair nature wed to human weal;
The rolling valley made a plain;
Its checkered squares of grass and grain;
The silvery rye, the golden wheat,
The flowery elders where they meet, —
Ay, even the springing corn I see,

And garden haunts of bird and bee;
And where, in daisied meadows, shines
The wandering river through its vines,
Move specks at random, which I know
Are herds a-grazing to and fro.

Yet still a goodly height it seems
From which the mountain pours his streams,
Or hinders, with caressing hands,
The sunlight seeking other lands.
Like some great giant, strong and proud,
He fronts the lowering thunder-cloud,
And wrests its treasures, to bestow
A guerdon on the realm below;
Or, by the deluge roused from sleep
Within his bristling forest-keep,
Shakes all his pines, and far and wide
Sends down a rich, imperious tide.
At night the whistling tempests meet
In tryst upon his topmost seat,
And all the phantoms of the sky
Frolic and gibber, storming by.

By day I see the ocean-mists
Float with the current where it lists,
And from my summit I can hail
Cloud-vessels passing on the gale, —
The stately argosies of air, —
And parley with the helmsmen there;
Can probe their dim, mysterious source,
Ask of their cargo and their course, —
Whence come? where bound? — and wait reply,
As, all sails spread, they hasten by.

If, foiled in what I fain would know,
Again I turn my eyes below
And eastward, past the hither mead
Where all day long the cattle feed,
A crescent gleam my sight allures
And clings about the hazy moors, —
The great, encircling, radiant sea,
Alone in its immensity.

Even there, a queen upon its shore,
I know the city evermore

Her palaces and temples rears,
And wooes the nations to her piers;
Yet the proud city seems a mole
To this horizon-bounded whole;
And, from my station on the mount,
The whole is little worth account
Beneath the overhanging sky,
That seems so far and yet so nigh.
Here breathe I inspiration rare,
Unburdened by the grosser air
That hugs the lower land, and feel
Through all my finer senses steal
The life of what that life may be,
Freed from this dull earth's density,
When we, with many a soul-felt thrill,
Shall thrid the ether at our will,
Through widening corridors of morn
And starry archways swiftly borne.

Here, in the process of the night,
The stars themselves a purer light
Give out, than reaches those who gaze

Enshrouded with the valley's haze.
October, entering Heaven's fane,
Assumes her lucent, annual reign:
Then what a dark and dismal clod,
Forsaken by the Sons of God,
Seems this sad world, to those which march
Across the high, illumined arch,
And with their brightness draw me forth
To scan the splendors of the North!
I see the Dragon, as he toils
With Ursa in his shining coils,
And mark the Huntsman lift his shield,
Confronting on the ancient field
The Bull, while in a mystic row
The jewels of his girdle glow;
Or, haply, I may ponder long
On that remoter, sparkling throng,
The orient sisterhood, around
Whose chief our Galaxy is wound;
Thus, half enwrapt in classic dreams,
And brooding over Learning's gleams,
I leave to gloom the under-land,

And from my watch-tower, close at hand,
Like him who led the favored race,
I look on glory face to face!

So, on the mountain-top, alone,
I dwell, as one who holds a throne;
Or prince, or peasant, him I count
My peer, who stands upon a mount,
Sees farther than the tribes below,
And knows the joys they cannot know;
And, though beyond the sound of speech
They reign, my soul goes out to reach,
Far on their noble heights elsewhere,
My brother-monarchs of the air.

HOLYOKE VALLEY.

"Something sweet
Followed youth, with flying feet,
And will never come again."

HOW many years have made their flights,
  Northampton, over thee and me,
Since last I scaled those purple heights
  That guard the pathway to the sea;

Or climbed, as now, the topmost crown
  Of western ridges, whence again
I see, for miles beyond the town,
  That sunlit stream divide the plain?

There still the giant warders stand
  And watch the current's downward flow,
And northward still, with threatening hand,
  The river bends his ancient bow.

I see the hazy lowlands meet
  The sky, and count each shining spire,
From those which sparkle at my feet
  To distant steeples tipt with fire.

For still, old town, thou art the same:
  The redbreasts sing their choral tune,
Within thy mantling elms aflame,
  As in that other, dearer June,

When here my footsteps entered first,
  And summer perfect beauty wore,
And all thy charms upon me burst,
  While Life's whole journey lay before.

Here every fragrant walk remains,
  Where happy maidens come and go,
And students saunter in the lanes,
  And hum the songs I used to know.

I gaze, yet find myself alone,
  And walk with solitary feet:
How strange these wonted ways have grown!
  Where are the friends I used to meet?

In yonder shaded Academe
  The rippling metres flow to-day,
But other boys at sunset dream
  Of love, and laurels far away;

And ah! from yonder trellised home,
  Less sweet the faces are that peer
Than those of old, and voices come
  Less musically to my ear.

Sigh not, ye breezy elms, but give
  The murmur of my sweetheart's vows,
When Life was something worth to live,
  And Love was young beneath your boughs!

Fade beauty, smiling everywhere,
  That can from year to year outlast
Those charms a thousand times more fair,
  And, O, our joys so quickly past!

Or smile to gladden fresher hearts
  Henceforth: but they shall yet be led,
Revisiting these ancient parts,
  Like me to mourn their glory fled.

THE FEAST OF HARVEST.

THE fair Earth smiled and turned herself and woke,
And to the Sun with nuptial greeting said:
"I had a dream, wherein it seemed men broke
A sovran league, and long years fought and bled,
Till down my sweet sides ran my children's gore,
And all my beautiful garments were made red,
And all my fertile fields were thicket-grown,
Nor could thy dear light reach me through the air;
At last a voice cried, 'Let them strive no more!'
Then music breathed, and lo! from my despair
I wake to joy, — yet would not joy alone!

"For, hark! I hear a murmur on the meads, —
Where as of old my children seek my face, —
The low of kine, the peaceful tramp of steeds,
Blithe shouts of then in many a pastoral place,
The noise of tilth through all my goodliest land;
And happy laughter of a dusky race

Whose brethren lift them from their ancient toil,
Saying: "The year of jubilee has come;
Gather the gifts of Earth with equal hand;
Henceforth ye too may share the birthright soil,
The corn, the wine, and all the harvest-home."

"O my dear lord, my radiant bridegroom, look!
Behold their joy who sorrowed in my dreams, —
The sword a share, the spear a pruning-hook;
Lo, I awake, and turn me toward thy beams
Even as a bride again! O, shed thy light
Upon my fruitful places in full streams!
Let there be yield for every living thing;
The land is fallow, — let there be increase
After the darkness of the sterile night;
Ay, let us twain a festival of Peace
Prepare, and hither all my nations bring!"

The fair Earth spake: the glad Sun speeded forth,
Hearing her matron words, and backward drave
To frozen caves the icy Wind of the North, —
And bade the South Wind from the tropic wave

Bring watery vapors over river and plain, —
And bade the East Wind cross her path, and lave
The lowlands, emptying there her laden mist, —
And bade the Wind of the West, the best wind, blow
After the early and the latter rain, —
And beamed himself, and oft the sweet Earth kissed,
While her swift servitors sped to and fro.

Forthwith the troop that, at the beck of Earth,
Foster her children, brought a glorious store
Of viands, food of immemorial worth,
Her earliest gifts, her tenderest evermore.
First came the Silvery Spirit, whose marshalled files
Climb up the glades in billowy breakers hoar,
Nodding their crests, — and at his side there sped
The Golden Spirit, whose yellow harvests trail
Across the continents and fringe the isles,
And freight men's argosies where'er they sail:
O, what a wealth of sheaves he there outspread!

Came the dear Spirit whom Earth doth love the best,
Fragrant of clover-bloom and new-mown hay,

Beneath whose mantle weary ones find rest,
On whose green skirts the little children play:
She bore the food our patient cattle crave.
Next, robed in silk, with tassels scattering spray,
Followed the generous Spirit of the Maize, —
And many a kindred shape of high renown
Bore in the clustering grape, the fruits that wave
On orchard branches or in gardens blaze,
And those the wind-shook forest hurtles down.

Even thus they laid a great and marvellous feast,
And Earth her children summoned joyously,
Throughout that goodliest land wherein had ceased
The vision of battle, and with glad hands free
These took their fill, and plenteous measures poured,
Beside, for those who dwelt beyond the sea;
Praise, like an incense, upward rose to Heaven
For that full harvest, — and the autumnal Sun
Stayed long above, — and ever at the board,
Peace, white-robed angel, held the high seat given,
And War far off withdrew his visage dun.

AUTUMN SONG.

NO clouds are in the morning sky,
  The vapors hug the stream, —
Who says that life and love can die
  In all this northern gleam?
At every turn the maples burn,
  The quail is whistling free,
The partridge whirs, and the frosted burs
  Are dropping for you and me.
    Ho! hilly ho! heigh O!
      Hilly ho!
In the clear October morning.

Along our path the woods are bold,
  And glow with ripe desire;
The yellow chestnut showers its gold,
  The sumachs spread their fire;
The breezes feel as crisp as steel,
  The buckwheat tops are red:

Then down the lane, love, scurry again,
  And over the stubble tread!
    Ho! hilly ho! heigh O!
        Hilly ho!
In the clear October morning.

WHAT THE WINDS BRING.

WHICH is the Wind that brings the cold?
  The North Wind, Freddy, and all the snow;
And the sheep will scamper into the fold
  When the North begins to blow.

Which is the Wind that brings the heat?
  The South Wind, Katy; and corn will grow,
And peaches redden for you to eat,
  When the South begins to blow.

Which is the Wind that brings the rain?
  The East Wind, Arty; and farmers know
That cows come shivering up the lane
  When the East begins to blow.

Which is the Wind that brings the flowers?
  The West Wind, Bessy; and soft and low
The birdies sing in the summer hours
  When the West begins to blow.

BETROTHED ANEW.

THE sunlight fills the trembling air,
And balmy days their guerdons bring;
The Earth again is young and fair,
And amorous with musky Spring.

The golden nurslings of the May
In splendor strew the spangled green,
And hues of tender beauty play,
Entangled where the willows lean.

Mark how the rippled currents flow:
What lustres on the meadows lie!
And hark, the songsters come and go,
And trill between the earth and sky.

Who told us that the years had fled,
Or borne afar our blissful youth?
Such joys are all about us spread,
We know the whisper was not truth.

The birds, that break from grass and grove,
  Sing every carol that they sung
When first our veins were rich with love,
  And May her mantle round us flung.

O fresh-lit dawn! immortal life!
  O Earth's betrothal, sweet and true,
With whose delights our souls are rife
  And aye their vernal vows renew!

Then, darling, walk with me this morn:
  Let your brown tresses drink its sheen;
These violets, within them worn,
  Of floral fays shall make you queen.

What though there comes a time of pain
  When autumn winds forebode decay;
The days of love are born again,
  That fabled time is far away!

And never seemed the land so fair
  As now, nor birds such notes to sing,
Since first within your shining hair
  I wove the blossoms of the Spring.

III.

SHADOW-LAND.

SHADOW-LAND.

"THE UNDISCOVERED COUNTRY."

COULD we but know
The land that ends our dark, uncertain travel,
Where lie those happier hills and meadows low, —
Ah, if beyond the spirit's inmost cavil,
Aught of that country could we surely know,
Who would not go?

Might we but hear
The hovering angels' high imagined chorus,
Or catch, betimes, with wakeful eyes and clear,
One radiant vista of the realm before us, —
With one rapt moment given to see and hear,
Ah, who would fear?

Were we quite sure
To find the peerless friend who left us lonely,
Or there, by some celestial stream as pure,
To gaze in eyes that here were lovelit only, —
This weary mortal coil, were we quite sure,
Who would endure?

"DARKNESS AND THE SHADOW."

WAKING, I have been nigh to Death, —
Have felt the chillness of his breath
Whiten my cheek and numb my heart,
And wondered why he stayed his dart, —
Yet quailed not, but could meet him so,
As any lesser friend or foe.

But sleeping, in the dreams of night,
His phantom stifles me with fright!
O God! what frozen horrors fall
Upon me with his visioned pall:
The movelessness, the unknown dread,
Fair life to pulseless silence wed!

And *is* the grave so darkly deep,
So hopeless, as it seems in sleep?
Can our sweet selves the coffin hold
So dumb within its crumbling mould?

And is the shroud so dank and drear
A garb, — the noisome worm *so* near?

Where then is Heaven's mercy fled, —
To quite forget the voiceless dead?

THE ASSAULT BY NIGHT.

ALL night we hear the rattling flaw,
The casements shiver with each breath;
And still more near the foemen draw,
The pioneers of Death.
Their grisly chieftain comes:
He steals upon us in the night;
Call up the guards! light every light!
Beat the alarum drums!

His tramp is at the outer door;
He bears against the shuddering walls;
Lo! what a dismal frost and hoar
Upon the window falls!
Outbar him while ye may!
Feed, feed the watch-fires everywhere, —
Even yet their cheery warmth will scare
This thing of night away.

Ye cannot! something chokes the grate
And clogs the air within its flues,
And runners from the entrance-gate
Come chill with evil news:
The bars are broken ope!
Ha! he has scaled the inner wall!
But fight him still, from hall to hall;
While life remains, there 's hope.

Too late! the very frame is dust,
The locks and trammels fall apart;
He reaches, scornful of their trust,
The portals of the heart.
Ay, take the citadel!
But where, grim Conqueror, is thy prey?
In vain thou 'lt search each secret way,
Its flight is hidden well.

We yield thee, for thy paltry spoils,
This shell, this ruin thou hast made;
Its tenant has escaped thy toils,
Though they were darkly laid.

Even now, immortal, pure,
It gains a house not made with hands,
A refuge in serener lands,
A heritage secure.

GEORGE ARNOLD.

GREENWOOD, NOVEMBER 13, 1865.

WE stood around the dreamless form
  Whose strength was so untimely shaken,
Whose sleep not all our love could warm,
  Nor any dearest voice awaken;

And while the Autumn breathed her sighs,
  And dropped a thousand leafy glories,
And all the pathways, and the skies,
  Were mindful of his songs and stories,

Nor failed to wear the mingled hues
  He loved, and knew so well to render,
But wooed, — alas, in vain! — their Muse
  For one more tuneful lay and tender,

We paused awhile, — the gathered few
  Who came, in longing, not in duty, —

With eyes that full of weeping grew,
  To look their lást upon his beauty.

Death would not rudely rob that face,
  Nor dim its fine Arcadian brightness,
But gave the lines a clearer grace,
  And sleep's repose, and marble's whiteness.

And, gazing there on him so young,
  We thought of all his ended mission,
The broken links, the songs unsung,
  The love that found no ripe fruition ;

Till last the old, old question came
  To hearts that beat with life around him,
Why Death, with downward torch aflame,
  Had searched our number till he found him?

Why passed the one who poorly knows
  That blithesome spell for either fortune
Or mocked with lingering menace those
  Whose pains the final thrust importune ;

Or left the toiling ones who bear
  The crowd's neglect, the want that presses,
The woes no human soul can share,
  Nor look, nor spoken word, confesses

And from the earth no answer came,
  The forest wore a stillness deeper,
The sky and lake smiled on the same,
  And voiceless as the silent sleeper.

And so we turned ourselves away,
  By earth and air and water chidden,
And left him with them, where he lay,
  A sharer of their secret hidden.

And each the staff and shell again
  Took up, and marched with memories haunted;
But henceforth, in our pilgrim-strain,
  We 'll miss a voice that sweetly chaunted!

THE SAD BRIDAL.

WHAT would you do, my dear one said, —
What would you do, if I were dead?
If Death should mumble, as he list,
These red lips which now you kist?
What would my love do, were I wed
To that ghastly groom instead;
If o'er me, in the chancel, Death
Should cast his amaranthine wreath, —
Before my eyes, with fingers pale,
Draw down the mouldy bridal veil?
— Ah no! no! it cannot be!
Death would spare their light, and flee,
And leave my love to Life and me!

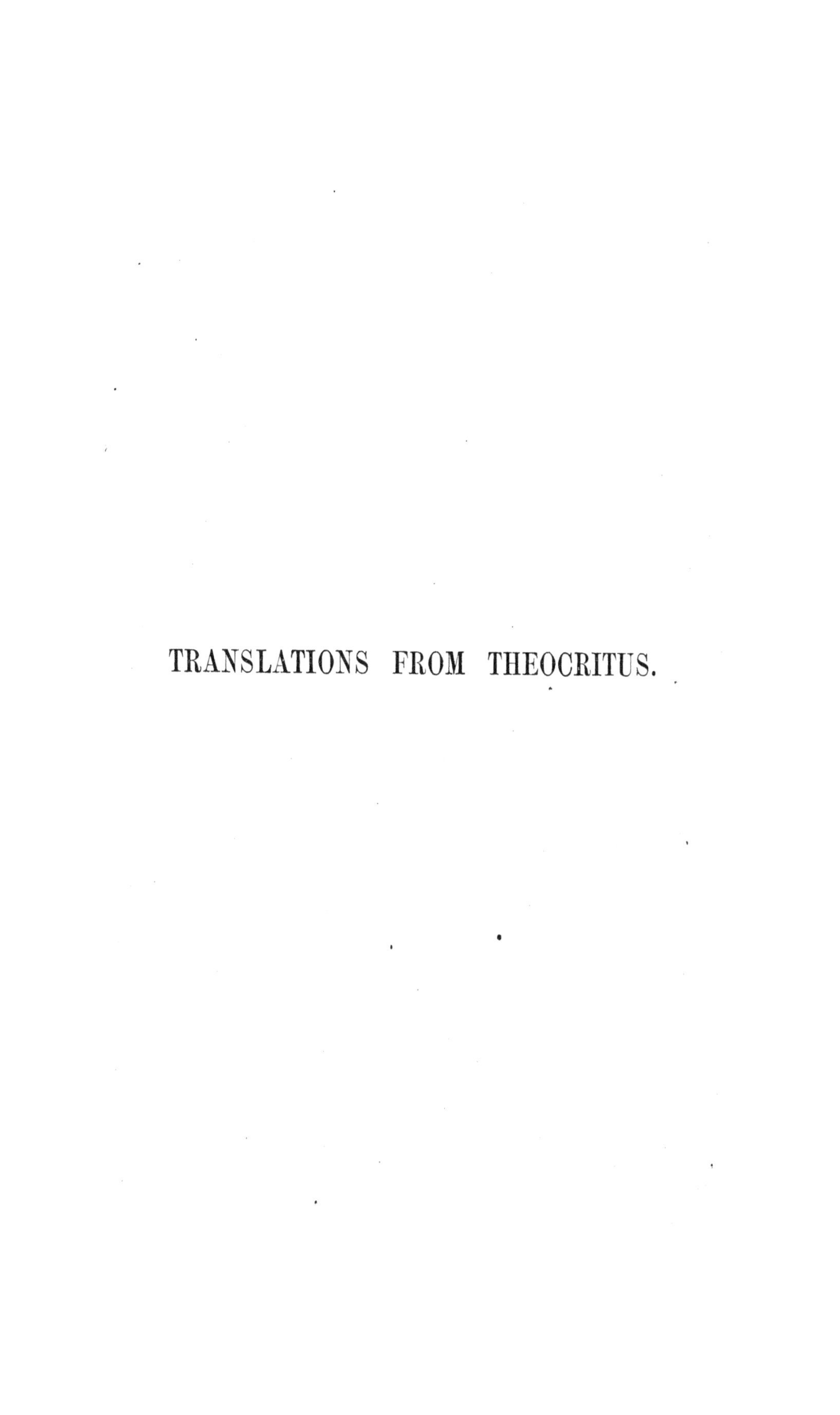

TRANSLATIONS FROM THEOCRITUS.

[*** A portion of the Tenth and the whole of the Thirteenth Idyls of Theocritus are given in the following translations. The text of "Hylas" is somewhat in dispute, and, as the translator has examined various editions, his version will be found to differ, in one or two places, from the common reading. He has, also, with good authority, divided the alternate songs of "The Reapers" into the couplets, which so exactly balance each other, and which are approved by critical and poetical instinct. The English hexameter has been selected as the only measure adapted to a literal and lineal rendering of the peculiar idyllic verse. These specimens of the Sicilian-Doric poetry, including a pastoral and a semi-epic theme, are from a version of the works of Theocritus, Bion, and Moschus, which the translator hopes to complete at some future day.]

TRANSLATIONS FROM THEOCRITUS.

THE REAPERS.

MILO AND BATTUS.

MILO.

BUT come now, down with the harvest!
Strike up also, I pray, a sweetheart song of the maiden;
Thus will you work more lightly:—I think you used to be tuneful.

BATTUS (*sings*).

"Sing with me, O Pierian Muses, the lass that is lissome;
For ye make all things fair, whatever ye touch, ye Divine Ones!

"Graceful Bombýcê, they call you a Syrian, scrawny and sunburnt, —
All but me, who alone pronounce you the color of honey.

"Ay, and the violet's dark, and the hyacinth wearing its letters:
None the less, for all that, are they sorted first in the garlands.

"She-goats hunt for the clover, the wolf goes after the she-goat,
After the plough the crane, — but I 've gone raving for you, love!

"Would that mine were as much as Crœsus, they say, was possessed of;
Then should we twain, in gold, be set up before Aphroditê;

"You with a — yes, with a flute, and a rose, or, maybe, an apple;
I, with new Amyclæan shoes, and a robe in the fashion.

"Graceful Bombýcê, your feet are pretty as dice that twinkle;
Soft is your voice; but your manner, — I have no words to express it!"

MILO.

Look you, the lad has been sly, composing us elegant ditties:
See how well he has measured the form of his even rhythm!
O this beard of mine, which I seem to have grown to no purpose!
But, to go on, now hear these words of the sage Lytiersês:

(*Sings.*)

"O Dêmêter, abounding in fruit and ears of the harvest,
Well may this field be worked and yield a crop beyond measure!

"Hard, bind hard, ye binders, the sheaves, lest ever a passer
Say, 'These men are poor sticks, and their pay is cash out of pocket.'

"Toward the north-wind let your swath of grain in the cutting
Look, or else to the west, for thus the ear will grow fuller.

"Threshers, threshing the corn, should shun the slumbers of noonday;
That is the very hour when the chaff flies off from the wheat-stalk.

"Reapers, begin your toil when the tuft-lark soars from the meadow:
Cease when he sleeps: besides, in the heat of the day take your leisure.

"Give me a frog's life, boys! he needs, to pour out his tipple,
No cup-bearer, not he, for 't is up to his mouth all around him.

"Better to boil the lentil, you 'll find it, niggardly steward:
'Ware lest you cut your hand in making two halves of a cummin."

(*Speaks.*)

Staves like these 't is fit that men at work in the sunshine
Troll; but, lad, 't were better to prate of your starveling passion
Unto your mother awake in her bed at break of the morning.

HYLAS.

NOT for ourselves alone the God, who fathered that stripling
Erôs, begat him, Nicias, as we have flattered us: neither
Unto ourselves the first have beauties seemed to be beauties, —
Not unto us, who are mortal and do not foresee the morrow;
But that heart of brass, Amphitryôn's son, who awaited
Stoutly the ruthless lion, he too was fond of a youth once, —
Graceful Hylas, the lad with the curling locks, — and he taught him
All fair things, as a father would teach the child of his bosom,
All which himself had learned, and great and renowned in song grown;

Nor was he ever at all apart from him, neither at midday,
Nor when the white-horsed car of Eôs ran up to Zeus-ward, —
Nor when the twittering chickens looked to their nest, and the mother
Over her smoky perch at eve had fluttered her pinions, —
So might the lad be featly trained to his heart's own liking,
And, with himself for guide, grow up a genuine hero.
Now when it chanced that Jason, the son of Æson, went sailing
After the Golden Fleece, and with him followed the nobles, —
Picked from all the towns and ripe for that service, — among them
Also to rich Iôlchos came the laboring hero,
He that was son of Alcmêne, — the heroine of Mideia;
By his side went Hylas down to the bulwarked Argo, —

Which good ship the clashing Cyanean rocks in no wise
Touched, but clove as an eagle, — and so ran into deep Phasis, —
Clove through a mighty surge, whence low reefs jutted in those days.
So at the time when the Pleiads rise, — and out-of-way places
Pasture the youngling lamb, and Spring has turned, — the immortal
Flower of heroes began of their voyage then to be mindful,
And, having sat them down again in the hollow Argo,
Came to the Hellespont, a south wind blowing, the third day,
And within the Propontis their anchorage made, — where oxen
Broaden Ciánian furrows afield, and brighten the ploughshare.
There stepping out on the beach they got the meal of the evening,

Two by two; and many were strewing a couch for them all, since
Close at hand lay a meadow, — to furnish sedge for the bedding:
Thence sharp flowering-rush and low galingale they cut them.
And with a brazen ewer the fair-haired Hylas was seeking
Water, for Hérаklês' supper, and sturdy Telamon's also, —
Comrades twain, that ever were used to eat at one table.
Erelong, too, he spied a spring in a low-lying hollow:
Round its brim there grew a host of rushes, and dark-blue
Celandine rose, and pale-green maiden-hair: and parsley
Throve, and the witch-grass tangling wild through watery places.
Now the Nymphs were starting a dance in the midst of the fountain, —
Sleepless Nymphs, divine, to country people a terror, —

Malis, Euníca, and one with her look of the Spring, Nychéa.
Soothly, the lad was holding the huge jar over the water,
Dipping in haste, when one and all grew fast to his hand there.
Love wound close around the gentle hearts of the bevy,
Love for the Argive boy: and headlong into the dark pool
Fell he, as when a fiery star has fallen from heaven
Headlong into the sea, and a sailor cries to his shipmates:
"Loosen the tackle, lads! — O, here comes a wind for sailing!"
As for the Nymphs, they held on their knees the tearful stripling,
And with their kindly words were fain to comfort his spirit.
But Amphitryôn's son, alarmed for the youth, bestirred him,
Taking Scythian-wise his bended bow and its arrows,

Also the club, which his right hand ever to hold was accustomed.
Thrice, ay, thrice he shouted HYLAS ! loud as his deep throat
Could, while thrice the lad heard underneath, and a thin voice
Came from the wave, and O, so near he was, yet so distant !
And as a thick-maned lion, that hears a whimpering fawn cry
Far away, — some lion that munches flesh on the mountains, —
Speeds from his lair to a meal which surely waits for his coming,
So, through untrodden brambles, Héraklês, craving the dear youth,
Sped in tremor and scoured great reaches this way and that way.
Reckless are they who love ! what ills he suffered while ranging
Cliffs and thickets ! and light, beside this, seemed the quest of Jason.

Also the club, which his right hand ever to hold was accustomed.
Thrice, ay, thrice he shouted HYLAS! loud as his deep throat
Could, while thrice the lad heard underneath, and a thin voice
Came from the wave, and O, so near he was, yet so distant!
And as a thick-maned lion, that hears a whimpering fawn cry
Far away, — some lion that munches flesh on the mountains, —
Speeds from his lair to a meal which surely waits for his coming,
So, through untrodden brambles, Hérаklês, craving the dear youth,